CLINICAL SUPERVISION

A Four-Stage Process of Growth and Discovery

Robert Taibbi

Families International, Inc.
Milwaukee, Wisconsin

Publishing in association with
Family Service America
11700 West Lake Park Drive
Milwaukee, Wisconsin 53224

Library of Congress Cataloging-in-Publication Data

Taibbi, Robert.
Clinical supervision : a four-stage process of growth and discovery / Robert Taibbi.
p. cm.
Includes bibliographical references.
ISBN 0–87304–281–6
1. Social workers—Supervision of. I. Title.
HV40.54.T35 1995
361.3'2'0683—dc20 95-36536

To my parents,
Vincent and Tina Taibbi

Contents

Acknowledgments

If our lives represent in some way the sum total of our relationships, being a supervisor and writing a book on supervision represent all my past and present relationships with my supervisors and those whom I have supervised. I am indebted to those who were gracious enough to teach me what they know and to those who have been kind enough over the years to let me be part of their own learning and growing process.

I want to thank Bill Johnson, my supervision groups for their interest and openness, and my colleagues for their ongoing support.

I especially want to thank Phyllis Colman for her willingness to learn alongside me over the years; for helping me shape my thoughts by sharing her own experiences; for her encouragement, support, and friendship.

Finally, a deep appreciation to my family—Rosemary, Chris, Jenni—for their steady presence, patience, and love.

Foreword

The meaning of *supervision* in clinical settings has evolved during the past half century. Originally understood as an educational process for developing knowledge and skills in clinicians, supervision now has a broader definition. The clinical supervisor is responsible not only for the educational aspects of supervision but also for administrative and supportive functions. The administrative function includes the supervisor's efforts to direct, coordinate, enhance, and evaluate clinicians' job performance in order to ensure that the work gets done effectively and efficiently. The supportive function includes the supervisor's efforts to sustain clinicians by offering emotional support and helping them deal with the day-to-day stresses, discouragements, and frustrations they inevitably experience. Given the complexity of the clinical supervisor's job, we have long needed a theory-based case-illustrated book on supervision that describes in understandable terms how the supervisor performs these three functions. Robert Taibbi has written such a book.

In *Clinical Supervision* Taibbi presents an integrative framework for understanding the supervisor's role and relationship with the clinician. The supervisor performs the administrative, educational, and supportive functions within the context of a positive interactive relationship with the clinician.

Taibbi discusses the nature of the supervisor–clinician relationship by describing the "parallel process," wherein the interaction between the supervisor and the clinician directly affects the relationship between the clinician and client. The parallels between the dynamics of supervision and the helping relationship have been noted by other authors. Taibbi, however, extends the concept of parallel processes. The model he develops provides a well conceptualized, easily comprehended framework for understanding the supervisory relationship as it develops over time. His articulation of the vertical dimensions consisting of six parallel processes and the horizontal dimensions of four developmental stages within each process provides supervisors with a useful means for conceptualizing their interactions with clinicians.

Taibbi's paradigm builds on sound tradition incorporating the notion of time and the concept of development in the supervisory relationship. Several developmental models of supervision have been described in the literature. These models emphasize the dynamic, shifting nature of the supervisor–clinician relationship as clinicians grow and develop professionally and ultimately move into a consultee–consultant type of relationship with the supervisor. Taibbi describes four stages of growth and development clearly and comprehensibly. His systematic approach to supervision "makes sense." His approach is comprehensive and useful to both supervisors and clinicians in helping them understand the evolving nature of their relationship.

Clinical Supervision is reader friendly. Taibbi brings theory alive with concrete examples and illustrations. His suggestions of supervisory tools and techniques are relevant, practical, and useful. Taibbi's book is based on more than knowledge of the literature; it reflects a practice wisdom emanating from his many years of experience as a supervisor and clinician. One realizes that Taibbi has "been there, done that." The writing style will delight the reader; the flow of thoughts and metaphors make this volume a pleasure to read.

Clinical Supervision makes a significant contribution to the literature on supervision by offering a systematic approach to a complex relationship. This book will be read and used by supervisors and clinicians.

Frank B. Raymond
Dean
College of Social Work
University of South Carolina

CHAPTER 1

The Life of the Supervisor

It's 8:30 A.M. and you have your weekly meeting with the other supervisors and the director, who begins with the bad news about the upcoming budget—at best a 2% increase in funding and no merit increases. The good news: if things go well, no staff cutbacks. Licensure people are coming in two weeks, she says. Let's get those charts up to date; we have no idea how many may be pulled. And be sure that every office has a map for escape routes in the event of fire. Oh, yes, a fire drill is scheduled for this afternoon at 2:00. Don't tell the staff.

Discussion is minimal, partly because the caffeine hasn't kicked in yet, and you and your colleagues aren't up to a long discussion. Better to pass along your comments in a note to the director or wait until you see her alone later in the week.

You get back to your office and find an urgent telephone message lying on your desk. Please call Mrs. Spi___—you can't read the rest and have no idea who this person is. You call the number and mumble Mrs. Spi___ to a child who answers the phone. The kid yells Mom into your ear, and Mom picks up the telephone clearly irritated. You identify yourself, and she begins her story. A client of one of your supervisees, she wants to be transferred to someone older who can better understand what it's like to have three children, two of whom are teenagers. You ask her if she has talked to the therapist about this, and she says no. You listen respectfully, and she asks if you could see her instead—she can tell that she could relate to you better. After 15 minutes you finally get off the phone. She has agreed to talk to the therapist about her feelings later that week. You write a quick note to the therapist summarizing the call and throw it in her mailbox.

You glance at the memo you found in your mailbox that morning—more stuff about the budget with a request for your input on areas for possible cuts. It's due by the end of the day. You peruse a spread sheet contrasting figures from the past three years with projections for next year. It looks overwhelming, so you toss it in your in-box and get ready for a supervisory session with one of your clinicians.

He's got a long agenda, but before he starts, you remind him about the charts and the licensure inspection coming up. He tends to fall behind, especially when he's feeling burned out, which you sense is the case right now. You broach the subject, but he shrugs it off. He sounds tired and probably should take some time off, but he also needs to get the charts completed. You tell him that.

He's anxious to talk about a particular case, an "awful" session with a couple that got out of control. The husband was ready to body slam his wife. The therapist stood up and yelled at the husband, who stormed out of the office. The wife cried throughout the rest of the session, saying that her husband acted like this at home all the time. The clinician wonders what he could have done differently to avoid this outburst, how he can reestablish a relationship with the husband. Good questions.

You ask the therapist to participate in an empty-chair exercise, imagining the husband in the chair. He's done this before and agrees. Within a few minutes you see the polarity that exists not only between the husband and the wife, but between the husband and therapist as well. A few minutes later, he sees it too, and even makes a link between the husband and his own father. He says he'll think about that, and you help him apply this insight to the next session. He feels better and you think you did a pretty good job.

The therapist leaves and you prepare quickly for a family case, one you've been working with for a while. While talking to the father a few minutes later, you keep thinking about what just happened in supervision. Have you been too easy on this father? What assumptions have you made about him? Deciding you need to practice what you preach, you take a more active role in creating changes in the room. The father fortunately doesn't storm out or body slam anyone. Although everyone feels a bit unsettled, there's more energy in the room.

Lunch time. You eat at your desk while staring at the spread sheet. You glance at a stack of job applications for the replacement of an experienced staff member who is leaving. The director has already determined how to use the money the agency will save by hiring an entry-level employee. Actually, the director would prefer to freeze the slot for a few months.

Another supervisory session—this one with the therapist of the mother you called earlier. You've confronted this problem with the therapist before—middle-aged clients who don't like a twenty-something unmarried therapist talking to them about raising kids. Actually the problem has come up less often as the therapist's self-confidence has increased during the past year. She takes the problem in stride and with a good sense of humor. She says that the mother may need some more individual support. She'll see her alone and talk to her about her personal needs. You remind her about the charts.

Fire drill! Clients mumble and complain, a few kids think it's fun, a couple of teenagers are glad to get out of their session, a woman says she won't pay for hers. Staff and clients stand together on the sidewalk outside the building. Everyone feels awkward. Fortunately, it's not raining.

Another case, this time with a four-year-old girl who has been abused. The play therapy is therapeutic for both client and therapist.

Your 4:00 P.M. appointment cancels. Thank God! You look at the spread sheet one more time, write a list of suggestions, and stick it in the director's box. One of the newer staff members sees your door open and asks if he can talk to you for a minute. He recently received a subpoena on a new case and appears overwhelmed. He doesn't talk very freely yet, even though his work seems pretty good. He's worried about the cross examination at the hearing. You tell him about your first testimony in court and try to give him some practical tips. He says he feels better, but you think he still looks shaky.

You glance at your watch—5:00 P.M. Mercifully, you don't have to work late tonight. With any luck, the traffic won't be too heavy.

The life of the supervisor

Not all days are like this one, of course. Some are better, some are worse. Nor are all supervisors alike—each has a unique mix of responsibilities, tasks, and supervisory style. But all supervisors, it's safe to say, wear several hats and feel pulled in different directions at any given time. This is what makes the work both interesting and, more often than not, frantic.

The supervisor isn't the only one who feels this way, especially in an agency setting. Others higher and lower on the organizational chart juggle various tasks at any one time—from the director, with her mix of personnel, budget, and public-relations problems, to the direct-line clinician consumed with thoughts about numerous clients, to the receptionist with six on the line, a fax coming in, and two clients in front of her who want to know where the bathroom is located.

This scenario seems to be the norm in mental health and social service agencies. They are, by definition, home for individual, family, and community crises, and everyone on the staff sometimes feels overwhelmed and burdened. No, supervisors aren't unique in the way they feel. What makes them different from their colleagues are their responsibilities, their skill, their place in the middle, and, most of all, their relationships with the clinicians for whom they are responsible.

The good supervisor

Do you remember your first supervisor? That woman you had in graduate school, perhaps, whose desk was always cluttered with shifting stacks of papers, who was always trying to quit smoking, who had a monologue for every question you asked. Or perhaps you remember a middle-aged man on your first job who reminded you of your uncle Bill or your brother Ted, who always cradled a coffee cup in his hands and was able to work miracles with angry, don't-want-to-be-here fathers. Or the twenty-something new supervisor, not much older than you, who always wore the same bluish suit and vacillated between acting tough and being indecisive. Regardless whether you remember your supervisors with affection, indifference, or contempt, they helped shape the professional you have become.

That's what supervisors do. Like parents, they leave their mark on us. They show us how to act or not act as a clinician. They teach us how to help others become more human. And when we become supervisors, our methods and skills reflect the sum of the supervisors we have had; they seep into our work. Although the remnants of bad supervisors may make us feel awkward or cynical or unsure of ourselves, the good ones guide us and guard us in our daily work.

The goal of this book is to show what it takes to be a good supervisor—the kind of supervisor who understands that supervision is more than checking charts, worrying about case loads and budgets, writing evaluations, conducting job interviews, or any of the other administrative tasks that agency work entails. A good supervisor is able to look beyond the mundane tasks and see the bigger challenge—helping other clinicians find their therapeutic voice, working style, and sense of who they are and want to be as a professional.

To do this, a good supervisor must be able to teach skills through the medium of practice knowledge, wisdom, and experience. He or she must be able to talk not only about the work, but about the self in the work. A good supervisor exemplifies the ideal therapeutic relationship through his or her relationship with the clinician.

This is what we will be exploring—the ever changing landscape of the supervisory relationship. The good supervisor, like a good parent or a good therapist, understands that change occurs within the psychological and physical space that lies between two people. The supervisory relationship provides a place of safety, an intersection where the professional and personal worlds meet. At this intersection, one discovers the power of relationship to change individuals as well as the power of individuals to change the relationship.

Professional and personal growth is the heart of supervision. Developmental theory tells us that growth occurs in stages; within chunks of experience and time we wrestle with core problems, try out new ideas, experience new feelings, and challenge those around us. Each stage becomes the foundation for the next. The clinician does not progress in a linear fashion; he or she jumps forward in levels, each level requiring new ways of thinking, mastery of new skills, and overcoming of assorted temptations and dangers. In this way, each level serves as the building block for the next level.

A good supervisor becomes a good guide who understands the developmental path that the clinician must travel. Using the clinician's behavior, thoughts, and fears as a map, he or she is able to pinpoint where the clinician is and to model the skills the clinician needs to remain emotionally and physically strong and self-confident in both work and personal life. By carefully reading and intuiting the clinician's progress and problems and by trusting in his or her own experience and instincts, the supervisor helps the clinician deal with the present terrain and prepare for what lies ahead.

Think of this book as a trail guide for supervisors, a way of knowing what's up ahead. We'll be following the path step by step, but before we start, we need to get our bearings by looking at the supervisor's and clinician's places within the agency. We'll start with the supervisor and life in the middle.

Avoiding the awkward middle

The middle can be a good place to be. In the middle one feels the comfort, warmth, and security that comes from being surrounded by others, like a child snuggled between two siblings on a cold winter night. Or there is the contentment that comes from the middle perspective—looking ahead at those who have advanced to greater opportunities, perhaps, but also greater responsibilities and looking behind at those still fumbling through life lessons that one has already learned. As Goldilocks discovered, sometimes the middle is just right.

But the middle can be an awkward, anxiety-producing place as well. Consider the problems of the middle child, often overlooked, wedged between the dictatorial oldest and the spoiled, whiny youngest. Or consider the problems of middle age, its "sandwich generation" smushed between the conflicting demands of aging parents and teenagers struggling with developmental issues.

It is here in the middle of the agency hierarchy that the supervisor lives. While many supervisors find it the best place to be, others have trouble adapting to the ambivalence and stress of the middle. To survive, they must develop their own ways of coping. One of the simplest is to become the go-between, a human soccer ball punted back and forth between the director and staff, the agency homing pigeon forever carrying messages between the two sides. Directors who don't like to deal with staff view this kind of supervisor as a real asset to the agency. However, such supervisors are poor role models for staff. Although he or she may avoid anxiety and conflict that result from independent action, this type of supervisor also relinquishes power and perhaps the respect of colleagues.

Other supervisors who don't like feeling like a bouncing ball can align themselves with one or the other side. Such a supervisor may become a "yes" person to the director, a parentified oldest child who doesn't make independent decisions but is good at carrying out the director's every command. This supervisor, too, may avoid the ambivalence of the middle, but once again at the price of authority and power.

It's tempting for naive or new staff to try to influence or impress this kind of supervisor in an effort to gain access to the director. They soon learn, however, that the supervisor values loyalty and compliance over creativity and innovation. More experienced staff are likely to bypass the supervisor and go directly to the director with their concerns.

For others, abdicating their leadership role and overaligning themselves with staff becomes the way out. Although staff may initially think this situation is great, eventually they realize that the supervisor is not really a supervisor, but merely an older or more experienced peer who lacks the power to advocate on their behalf.

Indecisive supervisors who can't decide which side or role to take take none. They emotionally and intellectually wall themselves off and often become rigid in their approach to work. Every situation, every therapist is reduced to the same problem, the same solution, the same reaction. This supervisor's tune is always the same, and the staff quickly learn it. Lacking leadership, staff may circumvent the superior with their concerns or, worse, become passive themselves.

The worst-case scenario is the supervisor who retires on the job rather than from the job. This supervisor goes through the motions, marks time, waits for his or her spouse to get a new job so they can move to New Mexico. He or she is out of the office a lot or keeps the office door closed or uses the workday as social time. Staff may go out to lunch with the supervisor and talk about vacations, children, or the latest movies, but real work and meaningful professional contact never occur.

Middleness and the good supervisor

The good supervisor is able to accept the middle for what it is—an ambiguous and ambivalent space in which roles and feelings are mixed. The good supervisor is able to use the anxiety inherent in the supervisory role for creative purposes, rather than turning it away. Instead of becoming reactive or passive to problems and conflicts, the good supervisor works hard to define the edges of his or her own professional identity, speaks out about things that matter, and puts values into practice. Instead of feeling lonely or resentful of the camaraderie among the direct-line staff, the good supervisor makes an effort to keep in touch with other supervisors in and out of the agency who can offer support. The good supervisor initiates actions rather than waits, synthesizes rather than merely repeats.

The good supervisor understands that the middle is a valuable and vibrant place where all sides and extremes meet. From this place, the supervisor integrates the divergent views and needs of staff and administration and serves as the medium through which the creative energy of the agency is funneled.

If you reflect upon past supervisors who made a powerful, positive impression on you, you will probably see how they affected not only you, but the agency environment itself. A good supervisor is the hub in the agency's wheel; he or she gives a sense of vitality and immediacy to the agency and the work it performs.

Life in an agency

Agencies vary in shape and size. Smaller agencies may have more flexibility but fewer resources; larger ones may be clumsy, cumbersome bureaucracies. Each agency must find its place in the community, define its mission, and establish its clientele and menu of services. Diversity and specialization is the name of the game; a mental health center is different from social services, which is different from family services, which is different from a university counseling center, which is different from a sexual abuse coordinating council, which is different from court services, and so forth. In healthy communities all these services interlock and coordinate with one another; in unhealthy communities they compete for resources.

But even in the best of times and the best of communities, most agencies are under considerable stress. Mental health has never been a high public priority in the United States, and most agencies are forced to scramble for funding. Licensing and accreditation requirements, although good for the public and for agencies, create periodic waves of additional stress for agencies. These internal and external demands for a system of quality control create the need for the supervisor role. Whereas the director stands at the door between the agency and the larger community, surveying the action on the street while balancing the books in the office, staff serve the clients seeking services. The supervisor stands in the middle, making sure the store is kept clean and that clients obtain high-quality service.

Easier said than done. The problems inherent in the supervisor's middle position are exacerbated in nonprofit or public agency environments. It's difficult to provide clients with what they want or need when the agency's shelves are bare or when staff are tired, harried, or distracted. Such concerns are supervisory concerns—juggling a growing case-load list, accommodating the community's increasing demands for services without adding staff, retaining overburdened staff while preventing burnout.

Staff turnover is a problem. When agency staff compare notes with their peers working in lucrative private practices with Thursdays off or begin to realize that not every client carries a gun or threatens to beat up the therapist, child, or spouse, they may begin drawing escape routes at their desk. When the supervisor passes these concerns on to the director, who has another set of financial concerns, the director may say that it's sad to see them go because we lose experienced staff, but we can always hire a less experienced person for less money.

As a result, many agency supervisors must deal with revolving-door hiring policies. New graduates view agencies as good places to get their feet wet, to obtain the supervision hours needed for licensure, but not as places where they will park their career. The work is hard, the pay is low. To compensate for a constant influx of inexperienced staff, the supervisor must devote most of his or her time to training, monitoring, and mopping up.

The supervisor and the director

Given these problems, a supervisor may be tempted to work toward becoming a director, from which position the agency's internal problems can be addressed from a more distant and seemingly more powerful position. Although in some agencies the supervisor is the power behind the throne, in well-functioning agencies the supervisor and director roles are separate but complementary. The director views the organization from the top, whereas the supervisor views it from the middle. Both views are critical to the long-term success of the agency.

A good director is a good leader who can promote the agency within the community. He or she brings the agency and community together, similar to the way a good supervisor brings administration and staff together. She or he negotiates and supports the internal world of the agency as well as the external world of the community. Great directors are able to create a vision that unites the agency and community in a common purpose.

Unfortunately, most directors are hired by boards made up of community members with varying levels of interest and expertise in the human service field. As the search for a director begins, board members may feel a sudden surge of importance, power, and responsibility. Board members who have been clocking in board time to pad their resumes, make new contacts, or fulfill their company's requirements for community service suddenly wake up and voice strong opinions. The autocrats and workaholics who have been pushing and pulling the board along for years suddenly find themselves going head-to-head with members whose names they can't remember. These internal problems can overwhelm a board and color members' view and selection of candidates.

Directors are generally hired to meet agency needs and priorities at a given point in time, and a search committee's list of screening qualifications generally reflects these concerns. If the agency is financially strapped, finding a good fiscal manager will be the number-one qualification. If the agency is interested in expanding its EAP base, finding someone connected to the business community becomes the priority. If quality of clinical work is thought to be going downhill, finding someone with a strong clinical background is viewed as important.

The problem with this approach, however, is that it takes a narrow view of the director's role. As long as the agency's immediate needs are met, the board–director–agency relationship functions well. If the needs change, however, as they often do, problems arise. For example, the director who gets the agency back on its financial feet may later have problems relating to staff. Or the EAP protocols deemed critical when the director was hired may move the agency rapidly toward a profit-margin, business mindset for which the director is not qualified. In such situations, the director must learn new skills and adapt to new needs.

Fortunately for most agencies, the situation rarely reaches a crisis point. Instead, most directors are destined forever to fight budget battles and negotiate community politics. Over time, their focus becomes increasingly narrow, their strengths increasingly specialized, their daily involvement with staff undermined by macro-level concerns. To compensate, they must rely on supervisors to keep the agency clinically afloat.

This scenario can make for a well-balanced team. While the director deals with the broader social and political issues that support or diminish the agency's ability to function, the supervisor focuses on the clinical environment of the agency.

Because the supervisor remains close to the ground-floor issues and perspectives defining the agency's work, he or she often becomes the keeper of agency tradition, history, culture, and collective memory. The supervisor remembers the monthly potluck, the agency's past work with a sister agency or a well-known family in the community, the types of staff training that have had a positive impact on staff morale and education. From the middle position, the supervisor introduces a new director to staff, orienting him or her to the culture of the agency, and also from the middle position helps translate the director's ideas and vision to the staff.

Thus the effective supervisor is an advocate, a storyteller, a buffer between staff and administration, a facilitator, and a translator. If the director has a strong clinical background, the supervisor prevents the agency's clinical orientation from becoming too narrow as a result of the director's clinical biases. If the director is a nonclinician, the supervisor translates clinical concerns into administrative language and administrative concerns into clinical language so that ideas from the top and bottom are readily communicated. The supervisor helps the director lead without drifting away from staff and helps staff articulate their needs and perceive the broader issues for which the director is responsible.

The new supervisor versus the old

The supervisor's level of experience is the final factor determining his or her position and authority within the agency. A new supervisor is like a new therapist, always playing catch up, having to develop work skills and style on the run. Pressure to perform creates anxiety during the early months, or even years, in the supervisory role, more often than not leaving the new supervisor feeling overwhelmed.

When I was promoted to supervisor two years out of graduate school, I was pleased for two minutes, then terrified. How could I pass on clinical skills to others if I was still learning them? How could I give advice on handling cases that I could barely manage myself? Feeling somewhat paranoid, I imagined that staff saw through my ignorance and deceit. I didn't ask my own supervisor for advice because I was afraid to put my incompetence on public record and thus forever be branded as a clinical dunce.

So I faked it. I attempted to meet my supervisor's expectations by giving the impression that I was in control of my staff. I tried to appease my staff by sympathizing with their concerns, nodding earnestly in agreement when they complained about the administration, and constantly referring them to the books I had (but hadn't read) in my bookcase. In a desperate effort to make myself look more mature and in control, I grew a beard, wore a suit, and carried a clipboard.

Such behaviors, I've come to realize, are not uncommon among new supervisors. Without adequate support or preparation from above, the new supervisor uses familiar methods of anxiety management. My method was appeasement. Others overcompensate for feelings of fragility by becoming drill-sergeant tough. Still others imprint like newborn ducklings on the first powerful staff person they see and imitate that person's every mannerism. This anxiety and paranoia will usually drop away before these coping styles solidify into a dysfunctional supervisory style, given a measure of support and luck.

But unfortunately some experienced supervisors have had neither. Without good, positive role models to demonstrate positive behaviors or emotional support to reduce the anxiety, the new supervisor can become an experienced, albeit dysfunctional, supervisor. Such dysfunction shows itself through poor communication, arbitrary rule setting, inconsistent boundaries, creating favorites and scapegoats, projecting one's anger and depression onto colleagues, and undermining the director's effort to lead. Beneath these negative behaviors lies poor professional self-esteem. The supervisor may feel a deep sense of incompetence and remain in constant fear that his or her incompetence will be exposed. Such supervisors not only become poor role models for the next generation of supervisors, but potentially they can spread dysfunction throughout the entire agency.

The way of the good supervisor

What separates the good supervisor from the poor one are the abilities to turn fears into opportunities and challenges and to remain open to change at the individual and organizational levels. The good supervisor learns to use the power inherent in the supervisory role, namely the power of intimacy and relationships. Although this type of power may not lend itself to the large-scale changes inherent in the director's role, it is capable of creating the simpler and perhaps deeper changes that occur at the individual level.

In *Habits of the Heart,* Robert Bellah (1985) discusses work and our relationship to it. He defines the job as our most basic, least committed relationship to work. We work at a job in order to make money, survive, and gather the resources we need that allow us to do what we love outside the workplace. The next level up is career. Here, we invest more of ourselves. We utilize our skills and talents to develop a path on which we travel for many years. The highest level of involvement with work is the *calling*, whereby we feel chosen for the work we perform. Who we are and what we do are intimately connected and of benefit to others. Our work and our life are inseparable. Work becomes sacred.

Supervisors, like all people, must take stock of their lives periodically, weighing whom they perceive themselves to be against what they do. A good supervisor is able to explore and reconnect the ties between the inner self and the outer work, between personal values or vision and what he or she does. In the process the good supervisor may find that the work is truly a calling and that the best way to measure ourselves and our lives is by the impressions we leave on the lives of others.

CHAPTER 2

The Life of the Clinician

Try the following exercise. Sit back in your chair and take a few deep breaths. Focus on your breathing. Feel the rhythm as you breathe in and out. Now imagine that you are entering a theater—a very large theater. As you enter, you notice a lot of people milling around in the lobby. You and they have come to watch a play. You walk through the lobby to the seating area and take the best seat in the house. In front of you is a large stage with a curtain drawn across it. You settle into your seat, and slowly the other people enter and begin to take the seats around you. The audience quiets, the house lights dim, and the stage lights come on.

The curtain rises and you see yourself when you were a child. You're with your parents. Something bad is happening or has just happened. Watch. Listen to what is said. Become aware of the set and scenery. Is anyone else on stage?

The curtain falls and act one is over. The curtain rises on the second act of the play. Again you see yourself, but now you're older—a teenager. Again your parents are on stage with you. Something negative and uncomfortable is happening. Again watch what happens. Listen to what is said. Notice whether anyone else is on stage.

The curtain falls then rises for the third act. You're a bit older. It's a time of change, a time for leaving. Perhaps you're leaving for college or moving to begin a new job, perhaps it's the day of your wedding. Regardless of the occasion, you're leaving your home and your parents. You're saying good-bye. What happens? What is said? How does everyone feel and act? Is anyone else on stage?

The curtain falls and rises for the next act. You're working at your first professional job, perhaps seeing one of your first clients or families. Again, watch and listen; be aware of the setting.

In the next act, you're in the present, at work, seeing a client or family. Watch what happens.

The curtain rises on the final act of the play. This time you are two years in the future. Again you're with clients. What happens? What is said?

The curtain falls, and the play is over. The house lights brighten, and the audience begins to walk out of the theater. You follow them out, hear them talking about the play. What do they say? How do you feel about what they say? Finally, when you feel ready, look around the room and refocus. If you wish, jot down your impressions.

You may have found this exercise easy to do or it may have been difficult for you to imagine the scenes. Perhaps your memories or feelings were fleeting and no pictures arose. That's fine. There's no correct way to do guided imagery. Some people find it easier to do than others.

The question one asks after any guided imagery exercise (or even after waking from a dream) is: Why am I seeing this now? Out of all the things that I could imagine, why am I imaging this today, and what, if anything, do these images say about me? The images that arise out of guided fantasies such as these are not prophetic or true in the absolute sense of the word. Rather, they offer you a different source of information about your life and your needs right now. If you were to perform the same exercise a few weeks or months from now, you would most likely see something very different. Although there's no "right" meaning for what you saw, the images and the feelings they evoke within you have personal value and meaning for you.

The first scene, from your childhood, is often representative of your feelings about your childhood. Were your parents arguing or yelling at you? Were you crying, quiet, or scared? Were both of your parents there or only one? Was anyone else there—a brother or sister? What was he or she doing? What was everyone talking about? What was the problem? What were you doing? How did you feel?

Adolescence is a time of change. What did you see in that second scene? What were you doing? Who was there? Were there arguments, laughter, silence? Who was missing? What was not being said? How was everyone feeling, and how did this scene compare with the first?

The third scene—leaving. It's been said that leaving, like other events in our lives, follows a pattern. Each of us learns how and when to leave. Often the leavings and separations throughout our lives feel similar to the way we felt when we first decided to leave home. What does this scene tell you about your own emotional bottom lines?

The world of work. Can you remember how you felt with your first client? Were you surprised by the way you acted? How has your work changed? How have your style and skills changed?

The future. Some people have a difficult time visualizing these scenes, especially if they are caught up in personal transitions. How have you, your work, your clients, the workplace changed or remained the same?

And leaving the theater. We are social beings and therefore interested in what others think about us. Others' perceptions of us help us see ourselves from a different perspective or cause us to compare our lives with the lives of those around us. How did you feel about the audience's comments as they left the theater? Did they like the play and the characters?

Consider the overall tone of the play. What themes emerged—conflict, being alone, hope, honesty, indecision?

Let the impressions that arise from this exercise linger and seep in over the next few days. Use the information in ways that feel helpful to you. We will be referring back to this exercise in the following sections as we discuss the developmental aspects of supervision.

The pull of therapy

Therapy is strange work. To sit day after day and listen to people describe their struggles, pain, and hardships, to have weekends interrupted by nagging thoughts about your client's comment as he left the office or by nagging phone calls asking you to bail him out of the latest emotional crisis—some jobs are certainly less emotionally draining.

Yet you, we, have chosen this work as our life's occupation. Why? Like all choices in our lives, our decision to become a therapist is rooted, at least in part, in the unconscious. We discover our life path in the contrast between our past and present, in the space between what we were and what we hoped to be, in things left unsaid, relationships unfinished or discarded.

I recently asked staff and colleagues their reasons for wanting to become a therapist. Here are some of their responses:

> *I basically enjoy helping others. I want to feel that I can make a difference in other people's lives. I think I'm good at what I do.*
>
> *I want to help heal relationships.*
>
> *I enjoy watching the inner processes of people, their behavior, seeing what makes them tick. I think at least part of me is some kind of psychological voyeur.*
>
> *I want to help others, but I know that at some level I want to help myself. I'm aware of the controlled intimacy of therapy.*
>
> *I want to help people change.*

It's hard to miss the theme here of helping others, specifically helping others to change and heal. This, of course, is what clinical work is all about—not merely hearing people's problems and hardships, but helping them make positive changes in their lives. Clinicians by definition are believers in and advocates for change; it is part of their own personal philosophy and faith. Some have experienced change through their own personal therapy or spiritual life, others through events in their lives. And a few who may feel stuck or frustrated making changes in themselves or their lives believe in it nonetheless, often transferring that belief to the client sitting in front of them.

But the belief in change is not the only pull upon us. As the responses suggest, subtler and deeper processes are at work. Out of all the occupations, why do we choose work that allows us to become involved with the dark and troubled sides of others? A sentence or two beyond casual conversation with your colleagues or a quick look back at the content of your imagery exercise may elicit an answer.

Research on the personal lives of therapists tells us that most therapists do not come from ideal childhoods of unconditional love and caring. Instead, we find a population of people who often felt different, lonely, apart from others, individuals who were emotionally leaned upon by a parent, usually a mother, and who learned at an early age to assume a caretaker role in the family (Guy, 1987).

What draws many into therapeutic work and what makes a good therapist is the ability to hold onto these pains of growing up, walking the fine line between repressing early experiences, which many in other walks of life have learned to do, and acting them out, as many others, clients and nonclients alike, do every day. The therapist enters the profession and the counseling room acutely sensitive to emotional pain and emotional life in general without becoming immersed in it. This ability to feel but not drown is what enables the therapist to build rapport, empathize with clients, tolerate and intellectually examine the cumulative pain of so many others. When combined with the therapist's faith in change, this becomes the support and objectivity that clients welcome and that makes the therapeutic process powerful and effective.

But if holding onto pain draws many clinicians into the field, the hope of healing those pains through others keeps them there. Again the research suggests that the pains of childhood seep into our adult lives as deep needs for intimacy and support from others; strong desires for power, influence, control; and the vicarious outlets that our clients and therapy can provide (Guy, 1987; Kottler, 1986). That ability to sense but keep that sensation at a distance, a skill we learned long ago to protect ourselves from the emotional insults of childhood, continues to make many of us gun-shy of strong emotional experiences.

As my colleagues' comments about psychological voyeurism and controlled intimacy suggest and as your own guided imagery may have shown, it often feels safer emotionally to step back from life by retreating into one's head—that is, to interpret, reframe, analyze, observe, watch, and talk—than it is to allow ourselves to become immersed in the murky waters of undefined feelings and actions. Through observing and talking, many of us express our anger, rebellion, regret, and sadness vicariously. Through others we are able to heal ourselves and cope with life.

Whereas for some therapists, doing therapy becomes a means of giving back the nurturance they received in childhood, for many others therapy becomes the safe means of getting what was not gotten. Working within the therapy process represents the best of all possible worlds—intimacy without risk, the feel of sharp-edged emotions that do not cut into our lives, the ability to control and remove ourselves from troubling feelings when we've had enough. This notion goes beyond the joke that the difference between clients and therapists is that clients need an hour of therapy a week but therapists need 40 hours. For many clinicians, therapy serves as a medium through which they discover their own inner life. These dynamics and needs may remain underground but emotionally charged until events in the therapeutic process bring them to the surface and they become part of the supervisory relationship and responsibility.

The agency as family

The personality characteristics that draw the clinician into the profession also draw a clinician to a particular agency. Each agency has a unique "feel" and "style" that one senses when walking through the front door. What is the physical environment like—the lighting, music, clutter, noise? Does the receptionist have a Big Mac or a single rose in a stem vase sitting on her desk? Does she call you mister or "Hon"? Does the director greet you in a pinstripe suit or tennis shoes and a cowboy shirt? The atmosphere carries over to the inner offices, where staff may yell back and forth through open doors or keep their doors closed and call their colleagues on the telephone. Regardless of the agency's style, however, the clinician must find a place within it.

How and how well the clinician can do this depends at least in part upon his or her own family experience. An agency's style reflects not only the leadership and culture of the agency but also the personality dynamics of the individuals who work there. Moreover these dynamics often reflect a cumulative family experience. The workplace has a natural propensity to create and recreate the dynamics of family life. The director becomes Dad or Mom; supervisors older brothers or sisters; direct line staff siblings with distinguishing personality characteristics, quirks, and ways of getting attention; adjunct staff aunts, uncles, grandmothers, and grandfathers. In large agencies, teams or departments split off into their own family groups with their own hierarchy, rules, traditions, tone, and style, making the large agency feel like a neighborhood or community.

The power of these dynamics should never be underestimated. A new staff member can stir up as much jealousy, role shifting, and suspicion as can the birth of a child into a family. A staff member promoted to supervisor may have to deal with the estranged relationships and resentments that their co-workers (siblings) feel regarding the "favoritism" shown by the agency administration (parents). When someone retires or leaves the agency, staff members may grieve the loss or engage in a sibling battle over who gets the bigger office or the room with the window.

How hard we battle, what roles we eventually assume in the agency family often stem from our own reactions to the roles we had within our families of origin. Whereas some desire to recreate their childhood families, others blossom in an agency setting that provides them with the family life they never experienced as a child. The only child finds in colleagues the siblings he never had. The one raised in a strict, military-type family and initially overwhelmed by the seeming "chaos" of the agency style is relieved when she realizes that she didn't have to fear unannounced inspections of her office by her supervisor; in this new environment, she finds permission to be creative.

The desire to "get now what we didn't get then" isn't restricted to work, of course; it percolates through all our adult relationships. But the workplace, with its wide choice of environments, camaraderie, and cultures, allows us to search out the environment that fits us. In extreme cases, the work environment may fit so well that marriage and family are pushed aside and the work family becomes the primary source of life satisfaction.

Even if we want something different, we usually start out by trying what we learned and know. The long-standing family comic instinctively tries out a joke at his first staff meeting to test the waters. If everyone laughs and the director doesn't frown, he breathes a sigh of relief knowing that the old shtick still works. Or the family intellectual may copy the latest study from the *Journal of Animal and Family Behavior* on crowding in rat societies and its implications for housing projects and pass it around to her co-workers with the note "Great stuff!" The family whiner complains about the scratches on his wall. The quiet one never asks a question or volunteers to speak. And the family rebel challenges every policy, procedure, or recommendation that comes down the pike. Dysfunctional agency systems may even have an agency scapegoat, the individual whom everyone ridicules and criticizes. The scapegoat is always on the verge of being fired, but for some reason never is. These matches of old roles in the agency environment create a powerful psychological contract for all concerned.

The difficult fit

But finding a good fit isn't always easy. Sometimes an individual's natural role is already taken by someone else. The agency's staff comic, for example, may feel challenged by a new staff member's first jokes. No one likes to be bumped, and something must give in the pecking order. The two may butt comic horns for a while, until a clear victor emerges. In my own family and in several jobs I've had, I fell into the "good son," "shining star" role. At one workplace, however, this role was already filled by an older man. At the point I considered leaving, my colleague moved away, thus allowing me to blossom in my natural role for a number of years.

In some instances, an agency's rules and culture may change suddenly and affect the established roles within the agency. An acquaintance who was a staff writer for a magazine told me that for many years the writing staff where he worked had a loose, interactive, eccentric quality to their relationships. He felt at home in this environment. Then his publishing company was bought by another company. A new editor took over, and suddenly writing became serious business. Notices were posted in the editorial area that quiet was expected so that the staff could concentrate on their work. The environment radically changed, and within a few months this writer quit.

Sometimes a person outgrows his or her workplace role. The agency's "little sister," for example, may get tired of being treated like the youngest sibling by her more experienced colleagues and desire more independence and recognition for her own skills and style. Similarly, the agency scapegoat may find ways to connect with others and no longer be willing to accept the blame of his co-workers. Stepping out into a new role can be difficult. The "little sister" may have to fight an uphill battle to gain the recognition and power that she feels she deserves; the scapegoat's behavioral changes may be overshadowed by his reputation and the role he has filled in the agency. In other words, the agency–family may not be willing or able to make the shifts that are required. In such cases, leaving the agency becomes the only option.

The self and the work

When Freud said that life consists of *lieben* and *arbeiten* (love and work), he suggested that the two concepts were distinct from each other. More often than not the two, however, are intertwined. To love requires work to sustain the love; to work well with joy and meaning is to love. Work is not merely something we do; it is something with which we have a relationship. Like any other relationship it is organic, tidal, developing slowly through discovery and self-reflection. The effective clinician, like the good supervisor, sees and appreciates this process in his or her life. He or she knows that as we move through the various stages of life, so too does our relationship with our work.

When a clinician speaks of a wish to have a good clinical experience in an agency, he or she is not merely talking about working on interesting cases or having the opportunity to learn new skills; rather, the clinician desires, but may not be able fully to articulate, an opportunity to discover, develop, draw tighter the connection between work and self. The agency becomes a place to do this work. Like the artist's studio, the agency is the space where the clinician can work with his or her medium and through that medium discover and develop the self.

In troubled agencies, the clinician is distracted from this process. Similar to the way that dysfunctional families drain the creative potential from family members, the dysfunctional agency with its rigid rules or instability disables the clinician's creativity. The clinician's personal engagement with work is never allowed to develop, and any enthusiasm for the job vanishes.

Good agencies, in contrast, support the clinician's relationship with self. The clinician feels welcomed and valued by staff and clients for his or her skills. Rules, although annoying at times, provide a sense of security and reduce the amount of time spent making trivial decisions. If rules hinder the work, they can be changed. In such an environment, the clinician feels at home.

The clinician and the good supervisor

The good supervisor understands the fabric of the clinician's world. The supervisory relationship guides the clinician through the agency, the work, and through the changing self. The supervisory relationship becomes the model for other relationships in the agency as well as for the inner relationship between the clinician's self and work.

The supervisor's task is to help the clinician fit in, to find a place, to see the agency as a home. The good supervisor is alert to the rules and roles but helps the clinician keep from becoming distracted by them. The supervisor helps the clinician to stay focused on him- or herself and to avoid the trap of comparing oneself to others in the agency. The clinician learns not to compete with everyone else but to focus on his or her own journey.

The good supervisor helps the clinician develop a therapeutic voice, discover a personal medium for self-expression, and clarify values, not only about practice and people, but about the place of work itself. The good supervisor accomplishes this task by nurturing the clinician's dreams.

Dreams about the self, about the future, and about the therapist that the clinician hopes to become give birth to the clinician's sense of work and keep it alive through difficult times. Just as the engaged couple naturally talk about their dreams before the wedding or as the couple in the broken-down marriage are drawn back to past dreams by their therapist, the good supervisor helps the novice clinician discover and articulate the dreams that lie inside and helps the burned-out, experienced clinician rekindle the dreams that once were. The good supervisor knows that work and the self come together in dreams, that beneath all the techniques, the assessments, all the practical functions and purposes of supervision, he or she is a midwife to the dreaming process.

CHAPTER 3

The Developmental Model: An Overview

The supervisor confronts two basic questions about the clinician at the beginning of the supervisory relationship: What does the clinician already know? What does the clinician need to learn in order to do the work that the job demands? The supervisor's educational assessment of the clinician forms the basis for setting training goals and insuring quality control. Because many agencies work with students and hire novice therapists, these questions are particularly important in the early stages of supervision. What knowledge and skills does the clinician need to work with the clients and the problems that the agency serves? Can the clinician work with sexually abused children or adults, alcoholics, clients with eating disorders and phobias, rebellious teenagers, borderline personalities, the chronically mentally ill? The wider the range of clients and problems, the broader the clinician's knowledge and skills base needs to be.

Much has been written in the literature, particularly in the family therapy field, about the value of "integrated" models of therapy (Duncan, 1988; Feldman, 1985; Lebow, 1984, 1987; Stanton, 1981). These models, which represent a more carefully planned eclectic approach, give the clinician a wider range of skills to handle the various types and levels of client problems. Having the flexibility to utilize the techniques and perspectives of several different theories increases the likelihood of finding an approach that works when another fails. If a structural approach with a particular family is having little impact, for example, the clinician might pull away from a family focus and begin psychodynamically based individual work.

This approach to supervision makes particularly good sense in the agency setting. Clinicians and agencies rarely have the luxury of focusing on a specific client or problem area. Even with specialization (e.g., children vs. adult services), the clinician providing such services is generally expected to be able to handle all the cases that come through. This across-the-board practice puts pressure on the clinician to know a lot about a lot. Given the often resistant, coerced stance of many agency clients, flexibility enhances the clinician's ability to engage and successfully treat various clients.

Flexibility is important for the clinician's professional development as well. Finding one's therapeutic style and voice requires a good measure of experimentation, exploration, and exposure to different clients and situations. Just as the good track coach will expose a talented but inexperienced runner to a variety of distances—sprints, quarter mile, half mile—in order to find the runner's strengths, the good supervisor will introduce the clinician to a wide range of clinical approaches. By putting theory into practice, the clinician is able to determine whether individual or family work, psychodynamic or cognitive approaches, directive or nondirective techniques, work with children or adults fit his or her personality, values, and natural talents.

Timing—what and when

What theories and skills should be taught and when should they be taught? Obviously, clinicians need to be able to understand, integrate, and use the information they receive. Many students and beginning clinicians begin work stuffed with information with little or no grounding in how to apply it. The best time to present information is when the clinician most needs it or is ready to hear and use it. Discuss the dynamics of child abuse when the clinician first begins work with an abused child, explore the issues of the middle stages of therapy as the clinician and client finish the assessment and settle in. All this is obvious.

But other sides of the issue of learning and timing are less obvious. Part of the supervisor's unique ability and role is to see ahead, to know what the clinician needs before he or she is able to articulate it. In order to do this, the supervisor needs not only to anticipate the content of the learning, but also to understand the clinician's own learning process. Working within this process, looking not only at the end but also the means of the learning forms an important part of the supervisory assessment and ongoing supervisory work.

Ekstein and Wallerstein (1958) in their classic text on supervision, *The Teaching and Learning of Psychotherapy,* describe what they call "problems about learning." Using a psychodynamic model, they describe various approaches or patterns that students take toward the learning process—learning by denial, learning by submission, learning by spoon feeding, discovering the problem. These different stances reflect the clinician's way of coping with the anxiety of the supervisory relationship while gathering the needed information. According to Ekstein and Wallerstein, the supervisor's goal is to help the clinician become aware of his or her learning approach, overcome its limitations, and thereby increase learning flexibility. In this context, the supervisory process, the working through of these problems in learning, becomes the learning process itself.

Appreciating and understanding the way these transference and countertransference aspects of the supervisory relationship affect how information is received by the clinician are important. But knowing the broader, more ordinary aspects of the clinician's learning process is also valuable. Does the clinician, for example, learn best by doing first and asking questions later? Can the clinician learn by reading or does he or she need to see it demonstrated? Is a lecture by the supervisor effective or is it better to focus on answering questions that the clinician brings in? Educators discuss these concepts in terms of adult learning styles, and neurolinguistic experts understand them as matching perceptual systems. Essentially, different mediums respond to different people.

However, the real answer to the question of timing and content in learning lies in the supervisor's awareness of both the vertical and horizontal nature of learning. One learns well not only by spreading information to fill intellectual holes and gaps, but also by moving information and knowledge downward so that it emotionally resonates in ways that tell the learner that these facts are true. Good clinical teaching addresses the psychological needs of clients as well as meets the specific developmental needs of the clinician and through the process ideally guides both to self-understanding. The good supervisor knows when it is time to push to help both reach new levels.

Parallel universes

These concepts are easier to see if we map them out. Based on Ekstein and Wallerstein's model, the following is a linear representation of the supervisor–therapist and therapist–client relationships:

S________T
T________C

The two relationships run parallel to each other, with the therapist representing the common link between them. The similarity between the relationships forms the basis of the concept of parallel process (Alpher, 1991; Ekstein & Wallerstein, 1958; Kadushin, 1992; Kahn, 1979). In the supervisory process, the therapist will sometimes identify with and act like the client. The supervisor's approach to the therapist models the way the therapist should approach the client. Good supervision trickles down to become good therapy.

The process can also move down from the supervisor. The therapist, for example, who perceives the supervisor as too harsh or confrontational may begin to treat clients the same way. By noticing these behaviors, the supervisor gains information about the way the therapist perceives the supervisor.

What we still need to add to these relationships is the horizontal dimensions—that is, the notion of time and the concept of development. Many developmental models of supervision have been presented in the literature (Simon & Brewster, 1983; Stoltenberg, 1981; Taibbi, 1990) and they all follow the same paradigms used in developmental models for children (e.g., Piaget, Freud) and for adults (e.g., Erikson). According to these models, the clinician moves through various stages, each with its own challenges, tasks, goals, and obstacles. Successful completion of one stage serves as the foundation for the next. Unfinished or poorly finished work in one stage can inhibit or weaken progress in the following stages.

These models help the supervisor perceive and organize the natural changes and growth in clinicians through the supervisory process. The on-line supervisor understands that the beginning clinician is going to sound and act very different from the clinician with five years' experience and that beginning clinicians will have similarities. Knowledge of the developmental process allows the supervisor to contour the supervisory relationship according to present tasks as well as anticipate future needs and problems. Such knowledge allows the supervisor to step back and see the bigger picture in order to help shape the relationship, goals, and focus of the supervision to meet the clinician's needs.

The developmental dimension provides us with a broad framework for matching educational needs with overall readiness. The clinician's professional development over time can be represented in a four-stage model as follows:

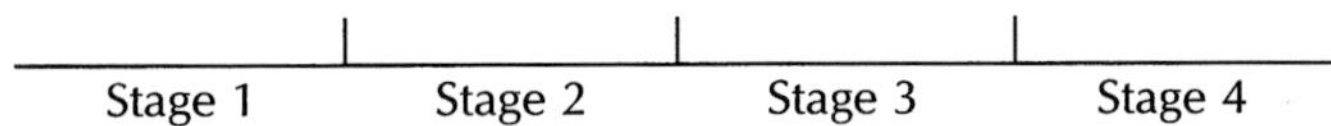

The model becomes more finely tuned when we place it in the context of the supervisory relationship. The stages of the clinician's development are observed and nurtured within the supervisory relationship to become part of that process.

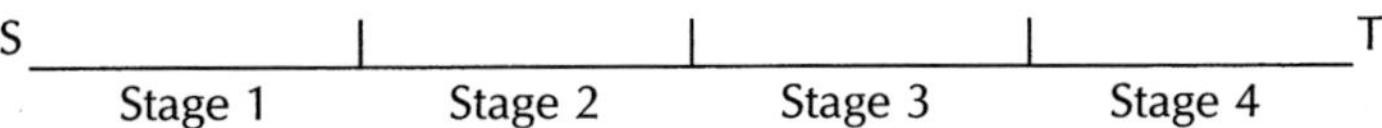

We now have two developmental tracks: the clinician moving through stages parallel with the supervisory relationship.

Clinical work follows the same time dimensions, moving through time and stages of therapy, each stage with its own changing needs and goals. Adding this additional parallel track, the relationships can be illustrated as follows:

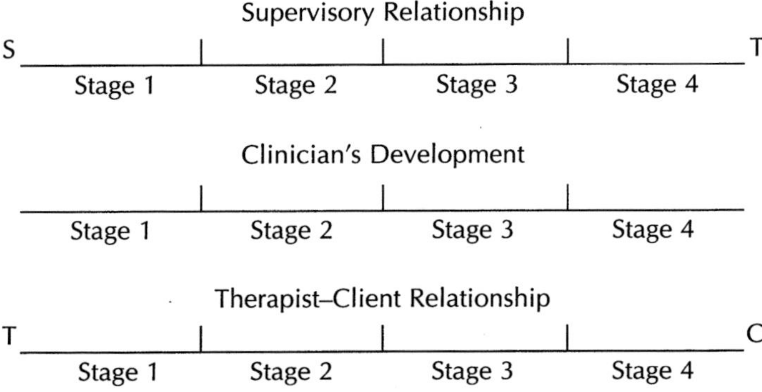

We now have three parallel universes. As the clinician moves through the stages of development, so too does the supervisory relationship and the clinician's relationships with specific clients. Issues from one universe flow into the others. Stage-one issues of starting out, for example, match stage-one relationships with supervisor and clients; clinicians' later needs to individuate from the supervisor and agency will be mirrored by clients individuating from the clinician. Good supervisory teaching addresses needs across all three universes.

But we also need to deal with the issue of emotional readiness. Just as clinicians ask themselves whether a particular client is emotionally ready to deal with a particular topic or problem, the supervisor must ask the same questions with regard to the clinician. As the clinician moves through each stage with a client, he or she is not only gaining information and establishing trust and intimacy, but is also moving through the client's history. This is the stuff of transference, the replication and perception of patterns in relationships over time. Similarly, as the supervisor moves through each stage with the clinician, the clinician's personal-history issues arise and are replicated along the way. Think back to the exercise in chapter 2—the parallels between our early years and adult years. Our personal history runs alongside the others and forms an additional parallel track.

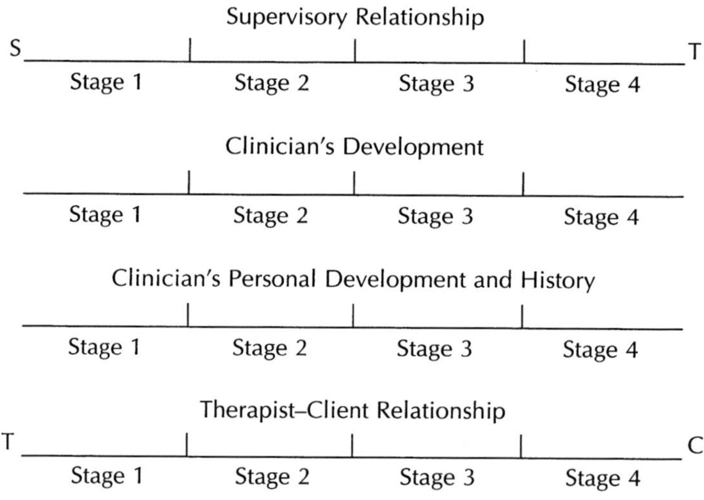

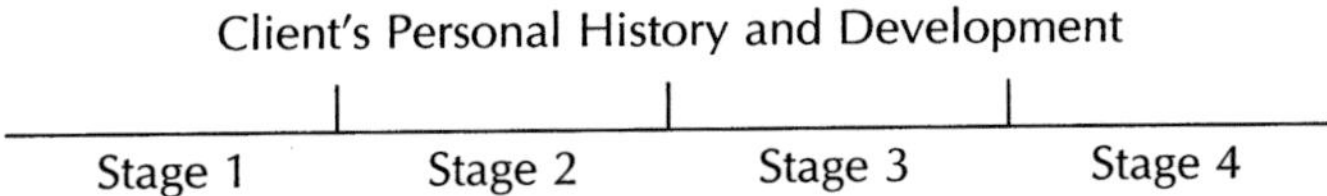

But there is still a final track to add—the supervisor's personal history. As the supervisor helps the clinician move through the stages, as issues from the clinician's past are stirred and brought into the supervisory relationship, the supervisor's personal issues are activated, forming the core of his or her own countertransference. The entire parallel system from the top down now looks like this:

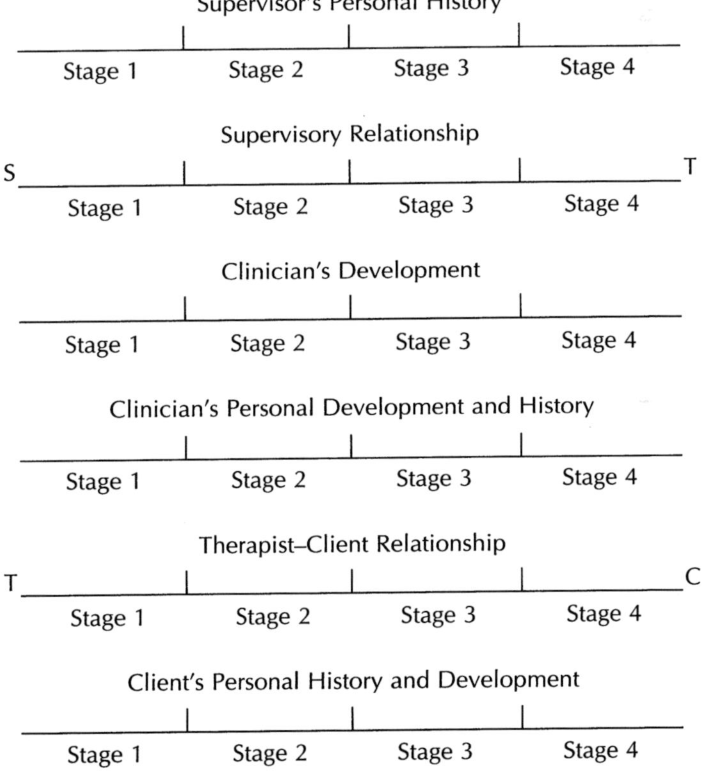

The learning process lies within both vertical and horizontal dimensions. Issues concerning what and when to teach, how to present information, how to shift from content to process and from client to clinician to supervisor all lie within this system of parallel universes. The truest questions generally begin with the client's own questions about his or her life or from within the therapy relationship and move upward to the supervisor. The truest learning moves down from the supervisor, incorporating the supervisor's self-awareness with his or her awareness of the dynamics of the supervisory relationship, the clinician's current need for information, and possible distortions in the supervisory and client relationship created by the therapist's own past issues. In other words, the best learning is learning that extends through all the various universes.

The developmental model

Easier said than done. It's impossible to have a perfect convergence of levels with each clinician during each supervisory session. As with therapy, those occasional near-perfect moments in supervisory sessions arise from the flatter plain of misses and partial answers, of powerful feelings left dangling without cognitive integration, of knowledge left floating without emotional grounding. When everything falls into place, it seems to occur by chance; in all likelihood such moments are probably guided by intuition and the quiet pooling of unconscious processes.

The goal should not be to strive for supervisory perfection, but rather to become aware of the various dimensions in which supervisory work can occur. When one door shuts on a particular level, the supervisor is able to move to another door on a different level similar to the way a family therapist shifts from family sessions to couples work or individual therapy. Again, flexibility, especially in an agency setting, is a valuable asset.

Nevertheless, the supervisor may feel lost negotiating the stairways of these vertical levels. The horizontal dimensions of the model help organize the process. By focusing on the characteristics of each developmental stage, the supervisor is given clues for what to look for and explore.

Table 1 presents a developmental model of supervision that incorporates the parallel dimensions and their characteristics. This four-stage

Table 1. Model of Clinical Development and Supervision

	Stage 1	Stage 2	Stage 3	Stage 4
Supervisory role	Supervisor as teacher	Supervisor as guide	Supervisor as gatekeeper	Supervisor as consultant
Themes	Establishing structure and competency, managing anxiety, safety	Reflection: past vs. present, self vs. others; dependence	Exploration, expansion, experimentation, counterdependence	Individuation, integration
Supervisory goals	Assess skills and coping style, insure quality control, reduce anxiety	Increase awareness of anxiety, parallel process, self in process	Increase awareness of strengths, values, intuitions	Problem solve, support professional and personal self
Supervisory methods	Observation of the supervisor, teaching, taping, reading	Co-therapy, live supervision, experiential methods	Group supervision, supervision by others, co-therapy, training programs	Supervisory training, expanded job responsibilities, advanced clinical training
Clinical approaches	Systemic thinking, structural, communication theory	Intergenerational, experiential, object relations	Strategic, NLP, hypnosis, psychomotor, cognitive and other adjunct approaches	Integrated model
Therapeutic themes	Managing chaos, establish structure, self as director	Long term vs. short term, inner process vs. outer, impasses	Anger, power, timing	Staleness, boredom
Dangers	Fear, rigidity	Overidentification with children and dependent clients, seduced by intimacy, burnout	Identity crisis, cynicism, overidentification with adolescents, seduced by power	Grief/loss

model covers the quality of the supervisory relationship, supervisory goals and methods, clinical training approaches, common therapeutic issues, obstacles, and overall themes for each stage, illustrating the unique aspects of each stage in the clinician's development within the workplace and within the supervisory relationship. Moving down the table, we see the vertical characteristics of the process and the elements that define each stage. Moving horizontally we see how change occurs over time as the clinician confronts new needs and challenges. Chapters four through seven explore each of these stages in detail. The following section, however, offers a general explanation of the map.

Reading the map

... STAGES

Like most developmental models, this one has four stages. It follows a scheme similar to a child's maturation process. Both the nature of the supervisory relationship, with its parent-like power and responsibility and the patterns that emerge around issues of dependency and separation lend themselves to this kind of replication. Again, it is this replication, the parallels between one's personal past and professional present, that ignites transference and countertransference issues.

The model, of course, represents an ideal; no person marches so smoothly through life's various stages. Although each stage has its own identifiable characteristics, the edges separating each stage are not always clearly definable. Regression can occur during periods of stress—a difficult case load, personal problems—and the clinician suddenly seems uncertain, confused, and more dependent on the supervisor.

... TIME FRAME

Sometimes we have a tendency to want to attach real time to the stages, to ground the stages in the real world (Dabney, 1994). The first stage, for example, seems to track the six-month clinician probationary period. The uncertainty of the new job and pressures to perform often fuel a clinician's fears and insecurities. However, settling into a relationship with a supervisor may take longer than six months. The supervisor, especially if new to supervision, may have personal anxiety to contend with, which may in turn stir anxieties in the clinician. Similarly the third stage suggests adolescent qualities of approach and avoidance, that is, periods of independence interspersed with short bursts of dependence. But it's difficult to place a time frame around these real-life issues. Confidence builds over time and depends upon experience, training opportunities, type of work, and the clinician's and supervisor's personal experience with individuation and grief.

One important variable is the level of experience with which the clinician starts. This model assumes new master's-level graduates for its starting point. But what about the doctoral-level psychologist with two years' experience, the bachelor's-level caseworker with ten years' experience, or the licensed MSW with five years' experience? Although different levels of education or experience may affect the time that a clinician remains in a particular stage, experience indicates that each individual moves through the various stages.

The only way the stages can be bypassed is when supervision itself is bypassed. If a new staff member with twenty years' experience is assigned to a supervisor with only a couple of years' experience, they may overtly or covertly agree to use supervision as an administrative channel but to skip the clinical focus. Such relationships can develop their own level of intimacy, but in a collegial as opposed to hierarchical way.

... CLINICAL APPROACHES

Consistent with the value of clinical flexibility and an integrated theoretical approach, this model uses a wide range of theories. Its starting point and foundation is family systems theories, theories well-suited to the variety of clients with whom most agencies work. They are able to address both the presenting problems and underlying dynamics across the family system in an efficient manner.

Of course, many agencies, supervisors, and clinicians favor other theoretical approaches, born from their experience within a particular community, tradition, training opportunities for staff, and graduate-school orientations. Regardless of the theoretical starting point, however, the goal remains to help the clinician develop a flexible approach to therapy that reflects his or her own therapeutic voice and values. The particular approach is not as important as is the timing of its presentation to the clinician. As the clinician moves through the various stages, the supervisor needs to ask him- or herself whether a particular theoretical approach will help or hinder the clinician's clinical and developmental tasks. A strongly confrontational clinical approach introduced in the early stages of the supervisory relationship, for example, might increase rather than reduce anxiety, inhibit rather than nurture trust. The new clinician, who feels stress at the outset, will feel more stress and may project his anxiety onto clients. The supervisor must consider the medium as well as the message in light of the clinician's developmental process.

... SUPERVISOR'S ROLES AND METHODS

Just as good parents are similar in what they do but different in how they do it, good supervisors find their own unique supervisory style while holding to the principles of good supervision. The roles and methods presented in Table 1 reflect the developmental needs and progress of the clinician, areas of supervisory focus based upon those needs, and tools timed for their maximum effectiveness.

Again, timing is important. Group supervision, for example, can be disastrous if all the supervisees in the group feel vulnerable and dependent upon the supervisor. They will be unable to use the group for support and will likely compete for the supervisor's attention. Group supervision works better for clinicians who are more confident and ready to individuate from the supervisor.

Similarly, the roles of each stage—teacher, guide, gatekeeper, consultant—reflect the shifting relationship boundaries as the clinician moves toward greater trust, independence, responsibility, and skill. The various roles suggest what to emphasize and when to utilize power but leave room for creativity in implementing these actions.

... THEMES, GOALS, AND THERAPEUTIC ISSUES

These form the heart of the developmental model, the parallels between clinician and client, clinician and supervisor, and the histories of each. As with other developmental models, the flow is from ambivalence and pseudo dependency, resulting from anxiety and distrust, to dependency, delving deeper into personal history, and intimacy. This work then becomes the foundation for the powerful issues of anger, power, and confrontation that arise in stage three, which if successfully negotiated allow the clinician to separate and move toward a peer relationship with the supervisor.

... DANGERS

Just as each stage has its own themes that tap into the clinician's personal needs, the fulfillment of those needs can seduce the clinician and impede progress. The dangers represent these seductions, the ways personal issues and inexperience contaminate clinical relationships, making them unbalanced and potentially dysfunctional for clinician and client alike.

Like any other map, this one helps the supervisor locate where he or she and the clinician are at any point in time and anticipate what is ahead. But the map is not the terrain itself. In the next four chapters, we will explore the landscape of each stage in detail.

CHAPTER 4

Stage 1: Beginnings— The Supervisor as Teacher

Susan starts each supervisory session the same way: "Let me tell you what happened with Billy at his last session." Sitting at the edge of her chair and looking at her pages of notes, she begins her play-by-play narrative. *He said, she said, he thought, she thought*—at a breathless pace. Finally she runs out of steam and story, takes a deep breath, leans back in the chair, and concludes, "I'm not sure what I should do next time."

Tom usually walks in the room with his clipboard in hand. On a white sheet of paper, you see the date, AGENDA written across the top and underlined, with several numbered items of client names and other topics. He talks more slowly than Susan and pauses every few sentences. "I had a good session," he often starts out, and then says a bit about what he observed in a family session or about some new information that one of the family members revealed. When he comes to the topic items, he usually asks broad questions—"Mrs. Johnson told me about this dream she had the other night. I've read some stuff on dream interpretation, but didn't know what to say about hers. In general, how do you interpret dreams? Are there any books you would recommend?" When I start talking he sits back, occasionally scribbles something on his clipboard, but usually appears to be half listening.

Stage one in the clinician's professional development—a new job, career, relationship with a supervisor, other staff, clients. Beginnings stir memories and emotions of other beginnings—the start of the new school year or moving into a new neighborhood, the awkwardness of new friendships, marriage, the birth of a child. Beginnings can elicit feelings of anticipation, optimism, dread, failure, adventure, or loss, but in general beginnings elicit feelings of anxiety. Everything has changed. The beginning clinician, like Susan or Tom, is no longer the student whose primary responsibility is a decent grade. Gone are the support of classmates, those long gripe sessions about professors and field instructors, the opportunities to compare notes and ideas with one another to avoid the embarrassment of asking "dumb" questions.

The new clinician suddenly has to earn his or her keep. It can be difficult trying to fit into the agency family, with its cliques, subgroups, and gossip. Everyone seems older and wiser, which makes the clinician feel younger and dumber. Six months' probation hang over the clinician's head with no second-chance make-up courses. Those deep-seated fears that you might not have what it takes to do this type of work may actually come true.

And the clients aren't much better. The clinician quickly finds major holes in his or her knowledge base. What exactly do you do in play therapy with a three-year-old who runs around the room screaming or seems more intent on eating the toys than playing with them? How do you respond to the woman who reminds you of your grandmother but says she thinks her husband of 40 years is gay? During a family session, it's hard to keep things on track—arguments break out, adolescents refuse to talk, and parents walk out shaking their heads saying that they could get the same help at home for free. Then some clients don't show up for their first appointment, or worse, for their second or third. You replay the last session over in your head, wondering what you said or did wrong. So many questions with so few answers. Doubt and guilt quickly set in.

Meeting and sidestepping the supervisor

Into this scenario walks the supervisor. The clinician is apt to study him or her carefully; initial impressions, reputation in the community, and stories from previous students set expectations and attitudes in motion. The supervisor is the arm of the agency—a new father or mother, or if young, an older brother or sister. But most of all, the supervisor is the boss.

"Welcome to the agency," the supervisor says. "If you have any problems, any questions, I'm the one to see. My door is always open to you. I'm here to help you. By the way, you'll be on probation for the next six months. At the end of this period, I'll do a formal evaluation to give you feedback on how I see you are progressing."

There's the catch: Come to me, trust me, tell me what you need, show me your problems, I want to help. But be careful, be competent, do a good job, or I'll fire you. It's like a cordial invitation to take a stroll through a mine field. The clinician who is told to be open and competent at the same time must decide which message is in his or her best interests to focus on. Do you hold back in order not to reveal your incompetence and perhaps appear resistant and uncooperative? Or do you confess your faults and fears and "prove" to the supervisor that you really are incompetent? Tough choice—similar to the bind the eight-year-old faces when his parent says, "Tell me the truth and the consequences won't be half as bad as they will be if I find out you lied." It's also similar to the situation of a client who must decide how much to reveal to an unknown clinician. In the absence of trust it's hard to trust. To make a decision the clinician remembers past relationships with other powerful people. Filled with anxiety, the new clinician attempts to balance honesty with self-protection by adopting one of several stances.

Susan illustrates one stance. Ekstein and Wallerstein (1958) refer to her stance as "spoon feeding" and Kadushin (1992) as the supervisee's "Woe Is Me" or "Little Old Me" game. She takes the easy and safe way out by asking the supervisor to do the clinical work; she becomes the messenger of higher clinical wisdom. This passivity allows the clinician to appear to be responsible without actually being responsible, to collect information without having to think about it. Again it's easy to see the parallel with clients who spill out their story of the week, then stare wide-eyed at the clinician waiting for advice. To complicate matters, the supervisor may be deceived by Susan's apparent honesty and openness as she spills out everything that happened yet know little about her larger self—how she thinks, feels, and knows. If they tacitly agree to take this supervisory path, they risk little. They avoid power struggles and obviate fretting over possible clinical disasters. Anxiety is reduced by walling off true thoughts and feelings.

Tom's stance is different. Unlike Susan, who is willing to risk appearing incompetent in the hope that she will fulfill the supervisor's need for control and power, Tom holds back, carefully tailoring the image he presents. Like Susan, he reveals little of himself, focusing discussion generally on the client. When he does refer to himself, it's to let the supervisor know how well he is performing. Questions, problems, and doubts are skimmed over or swallowed up in theoretical, global, fact-finding questions, like the one about dreams. Tom plays the role of graduate student, gathering information in a nonthreatening, noninteractive way. He asks interesting questions; for extra credit, he admires the supervisor's expertise. Through his complex weaving of questions and selected comments, he controls the supervisory session. Once he has set the supervisor off and running, he can lean back and take a nap.

Other variations are possible. For example, a new clinician may attempt to reduce anxiety by becoming personal—"I'm sorry I'm late. You wouldn't believe what my little boy did this morning. You have older kids, don't you?" Here the clinician is saying two things: "Let's talk about ourselves rather than about my work" and "If we get to know each other personally, maybe I can trust you." For others the leap into therapy is easier than the one into supervision. "I don't know what to do here because—I almost feel shaky talking about it (deep breath)—you see, I, like my client, was raised by wolves and haven't yet been able to work through my own deep-seated fears of forest fires, hunter's caps, or the color blaze orange." This clinician is more comfortable as a client and sidesteps clinical learning and risk taking by seducing the supervisor into being a therapist instead of a supervisor. Finally, some clinicians attempt to save face by questioning and arguing about everything the supervisor suggests, even though they eventually use the supervisor's suggestions. Ekstein and Wallerstein (1958) refer to this as "learning by vigorously denying." This stance often occurs in a later stage of the supervisory process.

Coping with anxiety

The above discussion and examples are not meant to imply that clinicians are manipulative or dishonest. They aren't. These stances are merely unconscious or subconscious ways of coping with the anxiety generated by an unfamiliar environment and the conflicting messages of the supervisor. By testing the boundaries of the relationship, clinicians compare and contrast this new relationship with past relationships in order to learn the rules and know how to proceed. The good supervisor needs to be able to detect these patterns early, separate real questions from distractions or controlling devices, and avoid the games, traps, and ploys that narrow the relationship into rigid roles and expectations. By weeding through this material as quickly and cleanly as possible, the supervisor discovers the clinician's overall tolerance for anxiety.

In *Coping with Conflict: Supervising Counselors and Psychotherapists,* Mueller and Kell (1972) describe three broad anxiety-coping styles: approaching, avoiding, and binding. *Approaching* is the willingness to move toward anxiety. Individuals who use this approach do not perceive anxiety as a problem in itself, but rather as a necessary ingredient of solving a problem, learning, or doing something new. Anxiety is recognized as a signal of growth and change; uncomfortable feelings subside as the new skill or situation becomes more familiar and is eventually mastered.

For the *avoider,* anxiety is not a natural step on the way to solving a problem, but represents the problem itself. This person feels overwhelmed, helpless, and stressed and has difficulty recognizing the problem behind these feelings or the solution that lies ahead. Avoiding the situation, suppressing feelings, and finding someone to take over become the primary goals.

Binders don't run away or run toward because they aren't even aware of their anxiety. Their secret weapon is control. They learn at an early age to cut anxiety off by controlling everything around them and thereby keeping anxiety-producing situations at a distance. In contrast with the approacher, who acknowledges feeling anxious but talks about solutions as well, or the avoider, who always looks flustered and "just doesn't know what to do next," the binder suggests an air of calm by steering conversations away from difficult topics; should the process heat up despite his or her efforts to control it, the binder will shut down emotionally.

It's easy to see how these styles can play off one another in relationships. Here are some possible combinations.

... APPROACH/APPROACH

Two approachers would, in theory at least, have the best of relationships. As changes develop, either one would take the risk to bring problems up and attempt to break dysfunctional patterns. Intimacy and creativity would develop naturally as they broke new ground and the relationship grew and changed.

... APPROACH/AVOID

The avoider may perceive the approacher as trying to make life miserable. Just as the avoider gets settled into a comfortable pattern, the approacher is likely to try something new or bring up a topic that the avoider would rather avoid or ignore. When problems arise, the approacher talks about forging ahead, whereas the avoider would rather lie low or retreat. For some avoiders, approachers are too overwhelming and they may leave the relationship. However, if the avoider can stick the relationship out and if the approacher is willing to discuss the anxiety he or she feels, demonstrate that it is not as deadly as the avoider believes it is, and help the avoider visualize the problem-solving process, the avoider may be able to look beyond personal anxiety and discover that action can bring mastery and increased self-confidence. Good parent–child, teacher–student relationships start with this combination.

... APPROACH/BIND

This is a difficult match. The approacher often feels stifled by the binder's control and by the routines or rationalization that represses the anxiety and tension in the relationship. The binder tends to perceive the approacher as foolhardy or impulsive and may use control to change or corral the approacher. Sometimes this combination is seen in client families, in which a rebellious teenager goes head-to-head with parents who are highly rational and subtly controlling. Such relationships often flounder. The approacher eventually leaves, while the binder shakes his or her head in pity or amusement.

... AVOID/AVOID

These two individuals tend to go around in circles as each scrambles to avoid anxiety. It can be very difficult to get this relationship off the ground. In new relationships, a mutual sense of helplessness and fear provides a common link. In long-standing relationships, stability is achieved through "protection pacts" whereby each protects the other by creating a distraction when sensing that the other is becoming anxious. For example, a husband in a family session might start complaining about his bad back immediately after the clinician asks his anxious wife about sex, or a child may knock over a bookcase when his mother begins to cry. A couple may have an unspoken list of anxiety-producing topics that they agree to avoid—money, a past affair, the death of a child, drinking bouts, or illnesses—and another more "comfortable" problem—Johnny's schoolwork—may be used as a way to decrease tension when these "taboo" problems surface.

... AVOID/BIND

The avoider may be seduced by the binder's sense of control and calm, thinking that he or she has finally found a person who can provide security and relief. Although this relationship may appear to function well for a while, eventually events or changes will disturb their relationship. The avoider may perceive the binder's control in potentially anxiety-arousing situations as pressure that increases his or her anxiety. The avoider's helplessness, for which the binder has no sympathy and little empathy or tolerance, causes the binder to exert greater control, which in turn creates more anxiety in the avoider. The avoider eventually leaves the relationship, often finding a new binder, with whom the relationship pattern is established again.

... BIND/BIND

This relationship can be stable superficially as long as the persons' areas of control don't overlap. On the surface, this relationship resembles that of the avoider/binder; however, it is a more sterile and intellectual relationship. The two parties lack the emotionality and anxiety-driven action that avoiders bring to the avoider/binder relationship. Binders prefer the stability of set routines and roles.

Anxiety and the clinician

So what does all this mean for the supervisor? A couple of things. First the good supervisor must be able to deal with, that is, approach, anxiety in the relationship. This is necessary to avoid stagnation among staff. In approaching and confronting problems, the supervisor serves as a good role model by moving the supervisory process and relationships into more challenging areas.

Second, good staff must also be able to approach anxiety in order to learn new skills, develop a professional self, and remain creative. A good clinician is able to think on his or her feet. Without this ability, the clinician is likely to become passive or controlling.

Approachers are easy to recognize, even during job interviews. They are able to talk openly about their anxiety and spontaneously about their emotions. They are aware of the stress of the interview itself and are likely to address these issues. Although they may start the interview stiffly or formally, within a few minutes their natural spontaneity takes over and they appear more relaxed. If asked a difficult question, they may think out loud, rather than give a pat answer. They are aware of their strengths and weaknesses. In a phrase, they have good self-esteem. The interviewer is likely to feel stimulated by the interview process.

Obviously, not all new staff meet these criteria. Many new staff act as avoiders in response to the stress of a new job. During the interview process, they vacillate between self-confidence and anxiety. On the job, they may be easily overwhelmed, rushing into the supervisor's office wringing their hands—"You won't believe what Jason just told me." If a crisis erupts, they may avoid returning calls from clients or put off appointments until they can get some advice, hoping secretly that things will blow over. If they can hook the supervisor into taking over and taking control, a relatively stable relationship may develop.

Binders give the initial impression of doing well under fire and in structured interviews may sound bright even if they don't seem very warm. Over time, however, their lack of spontaneity becomes apparent. In sessions they tend to have a list of questions on paper or in their heads, and nothing short of an earthquake will derail them from their agenda. Clients will be quietly ignored if their issues aren't linked to what the clinician wants to pursue. Many clients like binders. Their steadiness seems reassuring, especially early in the therapeutic process, until they realize that they are not being listened to.

In supervision they act like Tom, keeping a tight rein on the supervisory process. If the supervisor asks a question about reactions, feelings, or makes any attempt to penetrate the defenses, the supervisor may hear the right words but will not feel the right emotions. If pressed harder, the clinician will steer the conversation toward a theoretical discussion, or if all else fails, claim to be confused. Fortunately, few binders make it through graduate school in social work. They are usually weeded out in field work or they decide that they disagree with some of the basic assumptions of the therapy process and shift to another career track.

Identifying a clinician's primary approach to anxiety is the starting point in the supervisory assessment. This assessment should elicit the various stances that the clinician might take in the supervisory process, providing the supervisor with fundamental information about the clinician's approach to learning as well as where he or she should focus attention. The supervisor should begin by answering these basic questions.

- Can this person take risks? Does he or she look forward to new experiences and challenges?
- Is this person aware of and able to acknowledge anxiety?
- Is this person able to solve problems and apply skills and knowledge in new situations?
- Can this person listen well to others and take the initiative in supervisory and clinical sessions without attempting to control the process?
- Do I feel comfortable with and stimulated by this person or do I feel overwhelmed, bored, frustrated, or closed?

The good kid: The need for trust

With the answers to these questions, the supervisor has a baseline from which to work. However, the supervisor needs to be careful not to jump to conclusions.

We might have been too harsh on Tom, for example. Although he seems like an anxiety binder in supervision, he many not act controlling with clients. Similarly, Susan seems to avoid anxiety in supervision by acting helpless and passive but may actually be more independent with others. In other words, in the supervisory process, clinicians may react to the power inherent in the supervisor's role.

If we look at the research and consider how many therapists learned at an early age to be a caretaker in their family, if you think back over your own imagery exercise or talk to colleagues about their family experiences, it's clear that most clinicians did not play the role of rebel in their families, but more often than not were the "good kids." Even though novice clinicians may differ in their ways of coping with anxiety, most of them share a learned sensitivity to following the rules, to avoiding rather than approaching conflict, that often leads to overaccommodation and "should"-driven overachievement.

The positive side of this childhood survival tool of being sensitive and alert to the desires of others manifests itself in adulthood as sensitivity and empathy toward clients. On the negative side, however, it represents a developmental delay. The caretaking child is a child who by definition learned to put others first. The "good kid" does what others want rather than discovering and meeting personal wants and needs. These inner needs don't disappear, but may be acted out vicariously in the clinical forum. They can also arise in the supervisory relationship and process. As the clinician moves forward through the various stages and as his or her own personal history is activated through the parallel process, these personal needs can be discovered and explored.

As the new clinician enters the probationary period and faces the supervisor's power and pressure to perform, acting passive like Susan or noncommittal like Tom can represent "good kid" ways of keeping the supervisor at bay. Unlike Susan and Tom's pseudo dependency or accommodation, true dependency, which is a prerequisite to true independence, requires a letting go, trust, intimacy, and vulnerability, all of which are initially frightening and unfamiliar.

Sorting it out: Life with clients

So how does the supervisor separate the clinician's general coping with anxiety from "good kid" reactions to the supervisor? To deal with this issue, the supervisor needs to look at the clinician's relationships with clients.

I've often been surprised when listening to an audiotape, watching a video, or hearing a clinician speak about a case during team staffing by the contrast between the take-charge person in the clinical session and the passive, helpless, quiet clinician in supervision. One clinician I supervised barely said a word in supervision for the first seven or eight months, but from all other accounts, including feedback from clients, he was doing a good job. Over time he was able to relax and bring that stance into the supervisory sessions. The supervisor wants to discover the clinician's basic stance—those tied to power will dissipate as the relationship develops—and the parallel process is an important tool in discerning what this stance is.

Ted, for example, was always quiet and reserved during supervision, but he consistently berated clients for not doing the homework he assigned. He would talk endlessly about their need to take responsibility for their lives. Even when listening to a tape, he could not hear how critical he sounded. When confronted with this issue, he stated that he believed his approach was appropriate.

Clinicians who are aggressive, intimidating, controlling, or scolding with their clients are cause for concern. Such behavior, especially in clinicians who are submissive to their supervisor, suggests that the clinician identifies with the aggressor—in this case the supervisor. The clinician, unable to deal openly with the supervisor's power, projects distorted impressions of the supervisor onto his or her relationship with clients. The clients end up feeling battered, similar to the way the clinician feels in his or her relationship with the supervisor. In such relationships, the clinician and client can assume the roles of persecutor and victim, respectively.

A clinician might also react to an aggressive supervisor by identifying with the victim. For example, even though twelve-year-old Mary may be skipping school, staying out till 3 A.M., or smoking dope at the neighbor's, a clinician colludes with Mary's court-ordered parents who "can't understand why the courts and school are making such a fuss." After a session or two, both clinician and parents agree that Mary's behavior is "isolated," that she has actually gotten much better in the past few weeks, or that the problem reflects particular "family values" that the clinician must respect. Questions regarding depression, sexual abuse, or drug addiction are avoided, even though the supervisor may suspect that Mary is at risk.

Although this approach may stem from the "good-kid" reluctance to confront others and stir conflict, it might also represent the clinician's reaction to a harsh supervisor. Rather than identifying with the aggressive supervisor, as Ted did, this clinician identifies with the victimized, misunderstood clients. The clinician treats the client the way he or she wishes to be treated, that is, left alone. In so doing, the clinician attempts to block the supervisor's direction by insisting that evidence does not support the supervisor's concerns. Failure to follow through, quickly taking the side of clients, and intellectual defensiveness should inform the supervisor that a problem exists in the supervisory relationship.

Supervisors who suspect that they are the source of either of these clinical stances must act quickly—not by reprimanding or criticizing the clinician, which only fuels the distortion, but by increasing support and demonstrating a more positive, gentle form of direction. Positive modeling, to which these clinicians are very sensitive, will then be transferred to the client–clinician relationship.

Most of the supervisory themes and patterns revealed through the parallel process are fortunately more benign than those discussed above. New clinicians often describe clients as being confused, overwhelmed, under a lot of stress, in the midst of difficult transitions, impotent, ambivalent, afraid, and in need of support. Supervisory sessions tend to focus on issues of establishing rapport and trust and sensing the client's fear. What the clinician is hearing, of course, is what he or she most feels.

Skills: Knowing how to think

But not all anxiety stems from the relationships, of course. The clinician may also be inclined to ignore twelve-year-old Mary's problems because he or she does not know how to deal with the problems. At this stage, the supervisor needs to discover the gaps in the clinician's knowledge and skills.

Generally, the clinician has more skills than he or she realizes. New clinicians, however, often feel inadequate, pressured, and worried about making it through the probationary period, and thus forget how to apply the skills and knowledge they have learned. Theories that seemed so clear and understandable in a textbook suddenly turn to gibberish when the clinician tries to apply them to a family with three hyperactive children in the process of dismantling the office. If the supervisor's or agency's theoretical approach is different from that of the clinician, the clinician may feel isolated and unsupported.

Many beginning clinicians have the same difficulty that brings many clients to therapy—they have trouble seeing a larger pattern that lies beneath a host of seemingly different presenting problems. Mrs. Jones's problems with an abusive boyfriend, her ten-year-old back-talking son, and a harassing landlord overwhelm her, and, in short order, her clinician. Within a few minutes of the initial session both are staring at fires that are burning on several fronts at one time.

The larger connecting issues and solutions—Mrs. Jones's need, for example, to decide what she wants and to act more assertively to get it from others—are missed, especially if the clinician has much the same problem. The client's crisis quickly becomes the clinician's crisis, one of many similar crises if he or she has a case load of multiple-problem families. The supervisor's task is not only to stop the parallel process by remaining calm and clear, but also to help the clinician see that Mrs. Jones's three separate problems are really variations of a single problem.

Another common problem for beginners concerns the issue of process versus content. Some clinicians become overloaded by clients' problems and the multitude of facts and circumstances surrounding these problems. Rather than separating the themes and metaphors from the facts, both client and clinician run the risk of becoming mired in them. Even when clinicians do realize that the problem is actually being played out in the room, they may not know what to do next.

Is Mrs. Jones, for example, not only unaware of her wants, but is she also, by acting passively, placing the clinician in the role of another powerful person who controls what she does? Is Mrs. Jones identifying with these powerful others in her life, replicating their abusive nature and thereby giving the clinician a way to point out and model assertive ways of responding? Does the clinician at times feel that he or she is being treated like the ten-year-old and feel tempted to argue back?

This kind of thinking can be difficult for the novice because it requires multilevel thinking that may not yet be integrated and clinical flexibility that may not yet be developed. Even when the clinician has a sense that the problem is actually being played out in the room, he or she often does not know exactly what to do next or lacks the power to do it.

Separating process from content is part of the clinician's larger world of dichotomies—assessment versus treatment, individual versus family, inner feelings versus outer behavior, environmental versus psychological problems—all of which may be perceived as being mutually exclusive. If the presenting problem is not a crisis situation, the clinician may want to extend assessment for several weeks—gathering history, observing, talking to collaterals. What the new clinician may not fully realize is that the interaction with the client is already creating change, that treatment begins with the first visit and runs concurrent with the assessment process, and that assessment merely fine tunes the therapeutic process.

This assessment-first approach often backfires on the clinician because the client becomes frustrated with the process. Many clients have not had experience with counseling; they often expect to attend a couple of sessions, get the advice they need, and leave (Taibbi, 1980). To be pelted for several weeks with questions about family and the past or be asked to draw houses, people, and trees or plow through genograms that seem to the client to have little to do with the problem at hand may seem like a waste of time to the client and merely confirm suspicions about the usefulness of counseling. If the client drops out, the clinician who felt that he or she was doing a pretty good job will feel like a failure.

Frustration and failure are further fueled by the clinician's own expectations. The clinician may view therapy in idealistic terms, that is, as an opportunity to relieve suffering and pain and initiate the healing process. Such ideals, although admirable, may reflect the beginner's untested hopes as well as a narcissistic wish to save the world. Idealism untempered by realism is a recipe for defeat.

To overcome their anxiety, many new clinicians take the path of least resistance by becoming a good listener. These clinicians talk about favoring a Rogerian, nondirective therapeutic model. They are more apt to let the client ramble on in therapy, viewing all this material as fuel for the assessment and as a way to build rapport and trust.

After a couple of sessions, however, if the client hasn't quit, the clinician has several notebooks filled with seemingly unrelated facts and feels overwhelmed. The supervisor needs to help the clinician sort through this material by linking appropriate material to a theoretical model and treatment plan in order to put the therapeutic process in motion.

The supervisor's job is to anticipate these patterns and behaviors in order to help the clinician relieve or confront anxiety. By helping the clinician balance ideals against the reality of the work, the supervisor reduces anxiety, fills gaps in knowledge and skills, relieves the clinician's feelings of incompetence, and, most important, enhances the quality of service. To provide this service, the supervisor needs to establish a solid foundation for the supervisory relationship through honesty, respect, and a healthy dose of humor.

Your right foot

The supervisory relationship starts with the supervisor's trust in his or her own skills and sensitivity. It starts by remembering the anxiety and pressures of one's own early days in the profession. Without empathy, the supervisor may project these experiences as a new clinician onto the clinicians he or she supervises—an "if I survived this, you can too" attitude.

New supervisors still fresh from such experiences are at greater risk of being too tough and controlling, which increases the clinician's anxiety, supports dysfunctional patterns, and inhibits trust, or, because of overidentification, too lax and unstructured, which leaves the clinician confused.

Finally, the supervisor needs to recognize the pressure to perform as a supervisor. Am I the right person? Do I really have the skills to be a good supervisor? The supervisory relationship begins with self-honesty and self-reflection on the part of the supervisor. This preparation sets the tone and pace of the relationship and serves as the template for the supervisor's, and eventually the clinician's, expectations for the relationship.

So what does the supervisor do in those first days and weeks? The following is a set of agenda items that may be addressed in the first several supervisory sessions.

Welcome the clinician to the agency. As with any relationship, the first step is to welcome the clinician to the agency family. Introduce him or her to the staff and the facility, then allow some alone time to set up shop.

Talk about the job. This has all been done as part of the interview process, of course, but the details may have been lost in the stress of the interview. The clinician may have questions that he or she was reluctant to ask during the interview. Talk about case load, types of cases, and the like.

Orient the clinician to procedures. In addition to handing the clinician the five-inch-thick policy manual to read, explain the charting procedures, how to handle billing, telephone protocol, locking the doors at night, and so forth. In other words, clear the details out of the way, so the clinician is free to focus on more important concerns.

Talk about supervision. Although this too was probably covered during the interview process, do it again. A short monologue about your overall style and philosophy and the intellectual underpinnings of your approach will help orient the clinician.

Talk about expectations. The new clinician, who is likely to be feeling anxious, needs to know what is expected of him or her—the number of hours of direct service, the time and frequency of supervision, the availability of the supervisor, what to do with crises, the supervisor's own priorities and measures of performance, and the formal measures of performance (evaluations, forms, tapes, and the like). State the rules as well as inform the clinician about guidelines that are subject to negotiation.

Discuss the double bind. The supervisor should acknowledge the conflicting messages that the clinician is hearing, that is, the offering of trust and support together with the responsibility to evaluate. The supervisor doesn't need to resolve the tension between the two, but merely to acknowledge it and the feelings that may be engendered.

One might say the following:

> *I realize that I'm giving you a double message here to talk about your clinical problems while knowing that you're on probation. I don't expect you to know everything or to be a perfect clinician; that wouldn't be fair to you. What I look for most is willingness to learn new skills, to approach rather than be hindered by your anxiety. I want to help you develop your own style and therapeutic voice. I realize that you may feel shaky at first, particularly with clients and families who present problems that you haven't worked with before. I will give you plenty of feedback about how I think things are going, and I'd like you to do the same.*

This approach invites the clinician into the relationship and lets him or her know that it's O.K. to make mistakes, that trying and learning is more important than appearances.

Talk about goals. This follows naturally from the above discussion. What would the clinician like to learn during the next six months? What skills would he or she like to develop or experiment with? What types of problems or clients? What does he or she want from the supervisory relationship? Even though you may get "not sure" responses to some of these questions, such questions seed the relationship and give the anxious clinician something to hold onto.

Ask about learning styles and problems, strengths, weaknesses, and ways of handling anxiety. Although you will get answers to these questions throughout the supervisory process, it's important to bring up these topics early. The clinician needs to begin a personal self-evaluation process as soon as possible. The answers may seem vague and uncertain or too set and certain. That's fine—they'll become clearer as the clinician moves into the relationship and clinical practice.

Open the discussion to general topics. The clinician is responsible for laying out for the client the range and limits of therapy. Similarly, the supervisor defines the boundaries and range of the supervisory process. Ask the clinician about fears, challenges, heroes, pet theories, worst clients, and so forth. During the first few weeks of the relationship, the supervisor defines that which is acceptable from that which is unacceptable in the supervisory process. If something important is left out—the clinician's feelings about powerful men and women, for example—it is difficult to initiate such discussions after the relationship is established. Again, the goal is to help the clinician feel open to talk about personal issues.

Dreams. Not the stuff at night, but the bigger ones that sustain us over the years. The clinician needs to know that the supervisor is dedicated to helping the clinician achieve his or her dreams. If the clinician can talk about personal aspirations and feels supported by the supervisor in them, the seeds of a trusting relationship are sown.

Talk about yourself. The medium is the message. During those first few weeks and meetings, the clinician should not feel as though he or she is being interrogated. Such an approach merely leads to defensiveness. The goal is discussion, as open a discussion as is possible. The supervisor needs to reveal him- or herself. Not to achieve false or hurried intimacy, and certainly not to wash out the hierarchy inherent in their relationship, but rather to help the clinician feel a level of trust and comfort in the relationship. Self-disclosure on the part of the supervisor helps the clinician see the person behind the role.

Invite the clinician to tag along. As part of orientation to the agency and to the supervisor, invite the clinician to attend meetings and consultations. Let the clinician observe one of your own therapy sessions. In so doing, the clinician receives a clear message that you are open and that you too make mistakes. Moreover, the clinician is able to see you in a variety of settings, which helps round out his or her impressions associated with supervision.

Check charts, listen to tapes. Checking charts lets you know how the clinician perceives cases and develops treatment plans. Charts provide information about skill assessment and quality control as well as help you keep the clinician from falling into bad paperwork habits. If the clinician tapes a session, listen to it. Often it's useful to have a clinician turn in a tape with a written summary of the session, listen to it outside the supervisory session, pass back written comments to the clinician, then talk about it at the next supervision. (Chapter 9 focuses more specifically on the use of tapes.) Resist the temptation to criticize the tape to death; on the other hand, don't simply hand it back with a note saying, "Thanks." In the beginning, however, the information in the tape is secondary to the goal of desensitizing the clinician to the observation process.

Provide feedback. Recent research on marital relationships has found that a 5–1 ratio of positive to negative comments is the right proportion to keep the relationship on track (Gottman, 1994). The same is true for supervision. The only way to offset the tragic scenarios floating through the clinician's head is to provide plenty of feedback, especially positive feedback. Such feedback might combine comments on a particular case with more formal summaries of overall performance.

Choose process over content. Early in the supervisory relationship, process is always more important than content; that is, how you say something is more important than what you say, and how you present yourself—both your feelings and ideas—is more important than the content of your presentation. Your goal should be to serve as a good role model. Be clear, honest, fair, open, consistent, respectful. If you are too blunt, stiff, intellectual, overbearing, critical, demanding, or vague, the clinician is likely to feed these same behaviors back to you and clients. Approach your own anxiety, not only to model the process for the clinician but to ensure that you do not fall into stale, rigid, lifeless, or defensive patterns.

All these activities and foci provide a solid start to the relationship and give the clinician a clear idea of both the supervisory process and the supervisor. But the supervisor's work is just beginning. Once the supervisor has assessed the clinician's stances and skills, it's time to tackle them.

CHAPTER 5

Beginnings II: Confronting and Challenging

It takes time for trust and openness in the relationship to develop and become a true support for the clinician. Nevertheless, the supervisor needs to begin work early on the clinician's preset ways of handling anxiety—the anxiety-avoiding and binding behaviors, the "good child" passive and controlling behaviors, the attempts to turn supervision into therapy. Such behaviors if left unchecked interfere with clinical learning and quality service.

Clinicians who are easily overwhelmed by anxiety need help to settle their sense of panic and to confront its causes. Good listening on the part of the supervisor will help the clinician ventilate most of his or her anxiety. However, the supervisor also needs to direct the clinician's thinking toward problem solving by helping the clinician recognize his or her anxiety-avoiding style.

Ellen, for example, enters a supervisory session visibly upset and emotionally overwhelmed by her recent session with a woman who revealed in detail a history of sexual abuse. Ellen has not worked with any sexual-abuse victims before and is distraught both by the content of what she hears and by the sense that the client has laid this enormous problem in her lap. What does the supervisor do?

First, the supervisor needs to help Ellen reduce her anxiety so she can visualize the problem more clearly. The supervisor lets her talk and ventilate, listening calmly until she begins to settle down. After some of the feelings are drained, it may be tempting to explore Ellen's personal reactions—what made her so upset, why did she feel so immobilized, how did she handle the session? It's too soon, however, for the supervisor to initiate such discussions. Leading her in this direction might stir emotional content that would overwhelm her again, make clinical planning difficult, and give the message that she needs to sort through her own personal issues before she can take clinical action.

Instead, it's better to help Ellen step back from her feelings and into the problem and her clinical role—asking what she knows about sexual abuse, what she thinks the client needs most—to help her focus on the larger clinical picture and the knowledge and skills she has at her disposal. If Ellen lacks information about sexual abuse, the supervisor can provide such information to help ground her. Once Ellen's cognitive side is working, the supervisor can ask questions about her personal reactions in order to help her see what triggered her feelings. This discussion may lead naturally to a more general discussion of Ellen's ways of coping with strong emotions in others, handling new situations, general reactions to abuse and power, and anxiety-coping methods. This discussion should be followed by developing a clear plan for work during the next session with this client.

By the end of the supervisory session Ellen should feel settled and confident that she can take a proactive rather than reactive stance in the next session, that she alone is not responsible for fixing the client or her problem, and that the client, like her, needs to begin to see the problem intellectually as well as emotionally. Ellen should be given information about the dynamics of sexual abuse or a list of resources to which she can turn. She should know what she did well and, through the supervisor's modeling, she should know both how she can help the client with the problem and how she can relieve her anxiety by looking beyond it.

Ellen's anxiety will not dissipate overnight, of course. The shift from anxiety-avoiding to anxiety-approaching behavior is a long process that is supported with increasing self-confidence. The supervisor's goal is to help Ellen stay focused on the problem rather than become distracted by her own reaction to it. Over time, with the supervisor repeatedly confronting her avoidance, Ellen will be able to recognize her patterns more quickly and, drawing on the modeling of the supervisor, begin to shift gears within the therapy session itself. Increased self-control during the session will fuel her self-confidence; support from her supervisor and success with clients will help her learn that anxiety is a signal of growth and challenge.

But what if Ellen always comes in and wants the supervisor to tell her what to do? Attempts to be spoon-fed information are handled by putting down the spoon. In this scenario, the supervisor needs to push the problem back to Ellen, to get her to say what she thinks about the case. Although this is usually met with "I don't know," the little-kid maneuver to sidestep responsibility and the risk of mistake, the supervisor must treat her like an adult in order to move her beyond emotional and intellectual paralysis.

If the supervisor refuses to solve Ellen's problems for her, Ellen will be forced to move in a different direction. The supervisor might ask Ellen to think through the case and return to supervision with specific questions. If she has trouble doing this reflection, the supervisor might try to help her sort out her fears from her knowledge, help her see that feeling stuck because one doesn't know what to do is different from knowing what to do but being afraid to do it.

Passivity with clinicians is similar to passivity in clients; the trick is not to get lured into taking over the session. By throwing the responsibility for solving problems back to the clinician and by encouraging and rewarding initiation and risk taking, the supervisor demonstrates to the clinician that it is better to take risks than to be safe or always right. If the supervisor is too critical about the clinician's work or ideas, the clinician is likely to worry about performance and remain passive. When rewards for risk taking are combined with openness on the part of the supervisor, the clinician will usually begin to take charge of situations.

Confronting controlling and binding behaviors

Controlling and binding behaviors generate the same kind of anxiety as avoidance and passivity but need to be approached differently. The supervisor needs to separate clinicians' efforts to look good in front of the supervisor from the more serious and generalized anxiety resulting from attempting to control every situation. Although true binders who are completely removed from their anxiety are rare in clinical work, many new clinicians will attempt to control specific situations in an effort to bind the anxiety they feel.

Whereas passive or avoidance stances try to draw the supervisor in, a controlling stance attempts to keep the supervisor away. The clinician presents only that which he or she wishes to present, drawing the supervisor into presenting long, impersonal pictures and agreeing with the clinician's rationalization. In order to avoid this trap, the supervisor must tunnel beneath these defenses, tap into the clinician's anxiety, and bring him or her back into the room and the relationship.

This isn't as hard as it may sound. The tricky part is applying the right amount of pressure to the clinician's defenses. If the supervisor comes on too strong and is too demanding or critical, the clinician feels invaded and fears that his or her incompetence will finally be exposed. In such situations, the clinician is likely to retreat, and a power struggle will ensue. A direct but gentle approach is best.

This translates into asking rhetorical questions: "Tom, I notice that you always ask general questions rather than specific ones. I wonder why." "Tom, it seems that you are doing a good job with this family, but do you have cases with which you are having some problem?" "When I listened to that tape I wondered if that mother didn't follow through with your suggestion because she needed something different." "Tom, it seems that you have a fairly tight agenda for the session. I wonder if you are nervous about it and whether that's your way of handling your anxiety."

These types of statements and questions let the clinician know that the supervisor knows that more is going on than is being made apparent. By not pressing too hard for an answer or sounding overcritical, the supervisor prevents the clinician from shutting down and gives the clinician room to come back with a more honest response.

The supervisor must be careful to avoid the parallel process of muscling control of the supervisory session; rather, he or she should model the give and take of open dialogue. Self-disclosure by the supervisor can be a powerful tool, especially when it is linked with opportunities to observe the supervisor in action and to hear the supervisor talk about his or her own mistakes. Such disclosure reduces the clinician's distorted view of the supervisor's power by demonstrating to the clinician that everyone makes and survives mistakes.

The supervisor's goal is to get the clinician to talk more spontaneously and openly about his or her work anxiety. Such disclosure can be approached slowly by encouraging the clinician first to talk about nonclinical, personal topics, for example, asking Tom how he is getting along with the staff, whether he likes the town, if he misses graduate school and his old friends. This kind of discussion expands both the range of the process and the relationship. Because a clinician like Tom is so hypersensitive to criticism it's vital that the supervisor stay quiet and listen when Tom asks a specific question, expresses an emotion, or talks about a weakness in a sincere way. In fact, Tom needs to be supported and acknowledged whenever he is able to move off his predetermined course.

The clinician, however, should not confuse self-disclosure and openness on the part of the supervisor with any breakdown in the hierarchical nature of the clinician–supervisor relationship; it needs to remain clearly defined, or the clinician's "little kid" fantasies of power will rapidly fuel feelings of omnipotence. The supervisor might require the clinician to provide periodically an audiotape of a therapy session, present a process recording, or allow the supervisor to observe a session so that the supervisor is able to evaluate the clinician's performances. When Tom misses Mrs. Walker's suicidal ideation, ten-year-old Billy's fear about seeing his Dad on weekends, or Ms. Edward's quiet resistance, the supervisor needs to state clearly and directly what Tom is missing. The supervisor should provide clinical reasons for his concern as well as recommendations based on the client's needs. By clearly focusing on the clinical issues, the criticism feels less like a reprimand or personal attack.

Every couple of months the supervisor should schedule an unofficial but formal feedback session, during which time the clinician can evaluate his or her performance. This session is a good time to highlight strengths, talk about clinical progress, ask questions about the use of supervision, provide impressions about the state of the supervisory relationship, and reset clinical and personal goals. The supervisor has the opportunity here to condense the issues and themes discussed throughout the previous weeks regarding the clinician's use of self as well as to lay out expectations for improvement. If the supervisor has worked to build a solid, supportive supervisory relationship, the supervisor and clinician should be able to agree on and discuss problems and concerns.

Supervision versus therapy

How therapeutic should supervision be? The answer to how much therapy is part of good supervision is generally found within the supervisor's own therapeutic model. Psychoanalytic therapy has always used the training analysis as part of its education model; a supervisor oriented to solution-focused therapy, in contrast, will put greater emphasis on skills. Each supervisor needs to make up his or her own mind about this issue on the basis of clinical and personal values.

On the basis of the multilevel, integrated family-therapy-based learning model presented earlier, the supervisor's task is to help the clinician see how and when use of self gets in the way of achieving clinical goals. If Susan's initial goal, for example, is to build rapport with Mrs. Jones, but she finds that she is clearly having trouble doing so, part of the problem has to do with her skills and the other part is reflective of their relationship and Susan's feelings about the client. The supervisor needs to help Susan sort through these issues to discover what in herself is keeping her stuck.

Questioning, role playing, or other experiential techniques might help Susan realize, for example, that she is having a hard time engaging Mrs. Jones because the woman is so critical, just like Susan's father. The supervisor doesn't need to help Susan work through her relationship with her father, but rather help her separate her feelings about Dad from her clinical work with Mrs. Jones and offer her clear guidelines for shoring up the relationship in the next session. Usually the emotional awareness that Dad is being projected onto Mrs. Jones is enough. If Susan still has difficulty following through with the recommendations, then something else is going on with regard to the client or perhaps within the supervisory relationship, and the supervisor and Susan will need to dig deeper into the problem.

Susan may have problems with certain personality types or cases, not only with Mrs. Jones, but with clients with similar problems or personalities. The supervisor needs to point out such patterns, help Susan think through particular cases in advance so she can be alert to the emotional triggers that are likely to fuel her countertransference, and support her efforts to seek personal therapy if she desires to do so.

The supervisor is like a team trainer who provides first aid if someone is injured in a game but leaves the real medical care to the physician. The supervisor's job is to help the clinician stay in the game or, if necessary, pull the clinician out. The supervisor's bottom-line goal is always to ensure quality work performance.

But what about the new clinician who wants to turn supervision into therapy? Again, the supervisor must determine whether the clinician is identifying with the client role, whether he or she sincerely wants therapy from a professional colleague, whether therapy represents a way to establish intimacy with the supervisor, or whether therapy is merely a way to avoid clinical challenges. The supervisor might ask the clinician directly, "John, I noticed that you've been talking primarily about yourself this morning. I appreciate your openness, but we're not talking very much about your case. I'm wondering whether it's easier for you to talk about yourself or whether you're really feeling that these personal concerns are getting in the way of your clinical work." If John expresses his desire for therapy or gives the impression that he feels that his personal issues are affecting his work, the supervisor can draw clear lines—he or she will help John do the clinical work, but John needs to find someone else to handle the personal-therapy issues. Supervisors who are lured into becoming their supervisees' therapist find it difficult both to back out of the role later and to evaluate performance fairly.

Learning and developing clinical skills

Ideally, the supervisory relationship is like home—a safe place to regather oneself and mull over the events of the clinical day or week. Although the relationship reflects clinical life it is not the same as clinical life. For new clinicians especially, the supervisor uses these opportunities to reflect and regroup by teaching, helping the clinician build up a knowledge base and develop new therapeutic skills.

What the supervisor teaches depends, of course, on the clinician's past training and experience; the supervisor teaches what the clinician needs to learn most. Most new clinicians need to learn ways to cut through the details that bog them down and push them into a reactive and/or passive stance. The new clinician needs information about broad skills and ways of thinking that can be applied to a large number of cases and that encourage the clinician to take an active role in therapy. The following is a list of the basic skills that the beginning systems-oriented clinician needs to know.

... LOOK FOR THE HOLES

The notion of growth, approaching one's anxiety and finding creative solutions to problems, involves moving into new territory. Change in therapy means finding the holes and gaps in the client's presentation and helping the client fill them. The clinician and client don't necessarily need to find and do what is right, but rather what is difficult.

For example, Mr. Smith brings in his fifteen-year-old son, Danny, who is acting out, and spends ten minutes ranting about Danny's behavior during the past week. What are the holes in this client's presentation? Mr. Smith doesn't mention positive attributes of Danny, the other children in the family, the mother, the marriage, or himself. He doesn't say anything about Danny when he was younger or allow Danny to present his point of view. After listening to Mr. Smith for a few minutes, the experienced clinician might begin asking questions about any of these other subject areas. In so doing, the clinician not only receives more complete information, but Mr. Smith is given the opportunity to think and talk about issues he hasn't thought about before. In other words, the change process is initiated.

The supervisor can help the clinician look for holes in the client's presentation by asking pointed questions. The process is like seeing negative space in art, that is, seeing the space between objects in works of art rather than focusing on the objects themselves. It takes some practice but can be quickly picked up. When the clinician gets anxious or unsure where to go in a session, he or she can look for a hole and move toward it.

... SEEING AND STOPPING NEGATIVE PATTERNS

Behavioral patterns are maintained because they are predictable and therefore less likely to produce anxiety. The new clinician usually worries that he or she doesn't know how to initiate a new pattern after the old one is stopped. Although the supervisor can help the clinician think through options, clients themselves generally initiate a new pattern of interaction after the old one is stopped. If Mr. Smith's ranting on about Danny is cut off, the interactions and emotional content in the room will necessarily change.

... COMMUNICATION

Beginning clinicians are often uneasy about having too many people in the room; they like working with individual clients because one client seems easier to manage than multiple clients. New clinicians often fail to realize that dealing with more people gives one more to talk about, more directions in which to move, and more energy for problem solving.

For example, if Mr. Smith came to the session alone and ranted about Danny's behavior, the clinician may learn how Mr. Smith feels, but he will have to work harder to shake up Mr. Smith's world view. With Danny in the room, the clinician can always ask Danny how he feels about the problem. If Danny shuts down, the clinician can ask Mr. Smith to talk to Danny and or to speculate on what Danny is thinking. In other words, the clinician's basic focus is to keep the communication open. When open communication is combined with filling holes and gaps and stopping dysfunctional patterns, the process and content change of their own accord.

... DETERMINING WHO OWNS THE PROBLEM

Discovering who has the problem is a basic skill that is often overlooked in the heat of a session. The clinician must not only break down the separate problems that clients present but determine who owns what problem. Mr. Smith's initial ranting may suggest that Danny is a "bad kid." On closer examination, Danny is a "bad kid" because he stays out late, doesn't do his homework, and talks back to his mother, all of which are separate but connected problems. However, these problems are Mr. Smith's problems. Because Danny doesn't view these behaviors as problems, he doesn't try to change his behavior. Danny's problem may be that his father yells all the time or he's worried that his parents will divorce.

Rather than taking the time to map out the lines of responsibility for and ownership of problems, the new clinician often feels pressured to jump in and arbitrate or mediate the problems as they are presented. However, this approach merely replicates what the family is already doing. Instead, the clinician needs to slow the process down by obtaining consensus about the various problems so that a therapeutic contract can be set.

... LINKING THE PROCESS IN THE ROOM WITH THE PRESENTING PROBLEM

Many clients who come to agencies enter therapy with unrealistic expectations about the process. They many not understand how talking about a problem with a stranger will help them deal with it in the outside world. For example, Mr. Smith may think it's ridiculous to be asked about his marriage when he has his heart set on complaining about his son. Nevertheless, the clinician needs to connect the presenting problem with other aspects of family life and what occurs during the session with life outside it. Establishing these linkages keeps the clinician on track and the client motivated.

... INTERPRETATION FOLLOWS EXPERIENCE

This follows on the heels of establishing linkages among problems and issues. New clinicians who aren't nondirective can easily become overdirective during therapy. They feel pressured to explain extensively and to deliver their insights and interpretations about the process to the client so that the client feels that the sessions are worthwhile. Although feedback and education are important, too much too soon is counterproductive.

It's easier for the clinician and more therapeutic for the client to move from experience to explanation than from explanation to experience. It's always better to create an experience by asking powerful questions that prick a client's underlying sadness, directing a father and son to solve a problem together or engaging a client emotionally before explaining, defining, or linking problems. Mr. Smith needs to move beyond talking about his frustrations with his son and begin to feel and express his worries and concerns so that the clinician can present ways in which Mr. Smith can transfer his frustrations into positive actions that will benefit both of them. The informational, intellectual process should summarize, ground, and clarify the experience in the room.

... THEORY AND THE BEGINNING CLINICIAN

The six tasks discussed above enable the beginning clinician to screen out distracting messages, reduce anxiety, remain focused, and begin to change the process and content of therapeutic sessions in ways that keep clients involved. All the clinician needs is a theoretical approach to organize content and observations. Structural and communication theories work well in helping beginning clinicians to manage process and content and prescribe clear tasks for clients. Moreover, these approaches seem particularly effective with many clients seen at agencies. Other approaches—paradoxical, strategic, long-term psychodynamic, or other individual-based theories—require the ability to step back, quickly assess parallel process, engage in multilevel thinking, take an active and powerful role, or make a commitment to long-term treatment, all of which may be difficult for the beginning clinician.

With more experienced clinicians who are starting at the agency, the supervisor will need to assess their strengths and style in light of the agency case load. A psychodynamic approach, for example, may not fit well in a short-term-, problem-solving-based agency and client population or in an agency that relies heavily on home-based services. The supervisor's challenge is to help the clinician build skills by expanding them into new and more practical directions.

Mix and match

Few agency settings have the luxury to allow the supervisory relationship to settle in before giving the clinician tough clinical cases. Thus the supervisor must mix relationship building with skill development and quality control. How this mix works out depends on the clinician, the press of cases, and the supervisor's style.

Generally those first few days of orientation and office set-up are a good time to establish quality supervisory time. The supervisor needs to get to know the clinician and begin assessing his or her anxiety-coping style and clinical orientation. After clinical work begins, supervision tends to focus on anxiety about particular cases and clients. It is the supervisor's responsibility to ask about the relationship, define themes and large issues of supervision, help the clinician obtain a broader view of the agency and the supervisor, and articulate values. If the supervisor fails to incorporate these issues into supervisory sessions, the clinician will quickly become myopic regarding clinical work. It is the supervisor's, not the clinician's, responsibility to make sure that the relationship stays open and doesn't settle into any dysfunctional pattern.

After the supervisory process is in place, the supervisor needs to focus on the clinician's principal weaknesses. If Tom's control is undermining the clinical process, the supervisor must work on it. Similarly, Susan's weak diagnostic skill with children becomes the first task in supervision with her. If the supervisor isn't clear about what to focus on first, he or she should ask the clinician.

Although education and skills development are by and large the major task and the most supportive and productive role for the supervisor during this stage, the good supervisor always tries to deal with as many vertical levels of experience as is possible. The good supervisor looks for ways to help the clinician become increasingly aware of the parallel process both in the room with the supervisor and with clients as well as aware of overidentification with particular clients or pockets of personal issues that inhibit clear clinical thinking.

These tasks are difficult at the beginning stage when anxiety is high and the relationship is still forming; the supervisor must avoid pressing too hard or the clinician may withdraw. Nevertheless, the supervisor can plant seeds for this type of thinking while gently pushing the boundaries in order to determine exactly where they are. Those special and rare times when learning touches many levels at once reflect intimate, ground-breaking experiences for both the clinician and supervisor.

Enemies and dangers

In *The Teachings of Don Juan* (1968), Carlos Castaneda describes his apprenticeship to an Indian sorcerer and teacher. Don Juan talks about the process of becoming a "man of knowledge" and tells Castaneda that he must defeat emotional and intellectual "enemies" in order to grow. If he fails to defeat any "enemies" his development will be stopped forever.

During this first stage, the clinician confronts two of these enemies. The first enemy is fear—fear of chaos, anger, confrontation, incompetence, failure, fear created out of the unknown. The clinician only knows what he or she doesn't know, and, as Don Juan says, "What he learns is never what he pictured or imagined." Such fear can hold the clinician back and fuel the anxiety that creates dysfunctional patterns with clients and the supervisor. If the supervisor is unable to help the clinician reduce anxiety and approach his or her fears, the clinician will become stuck in this stage. Even though the clinician may continue to gather information, real clinical and personal growth and the discovery of a therapeutic voice will not be possible. Over time these individuals are likely to become bored with the work and move onto something else.

The cousin of fear and the second enemy that can dominate this stage is rigidity. Rigidity creates tunnel vision and control, shielding the clinician from confronting new situations and potential change. For example, the clinician may seize upon some concept—enmeshment, triangulation, repressed anger—or some interview format that reduces each session and each client to the same formula and process. Obviously, clinicians who cannot overcome this enemy also stop growing. The supervisor is responsible for recognizing these patterns and preventing the clinician from falling into these personal and professional ruts.

Of course, the supervisor faces the same enemies. If the supervisor is afraid to supervise, engage, challenge, reach out, and self-disclose, the relationship is stopped in its tracks. Similarly, if the supervisor becomes rigid and reductionistic and begins treating all supervisees the same way, true supervision is lost.

Other dangers also exist. Lack of attention, timing, and pacing, although not as incapacitating as fear and rigidity, can also trip the supervisor or clinician. Not screening cases carefully enough, not orienting the clinician properly, being too intrusive or distant, loading the clinician with too many cases too soon, not helping the clinician find a place within the agency family—all of these can inhibit the relationship and create emotional overload that makes learning difficult, hurts client service, and hampers adjustment to the work environment.

Making the difficult decisions

What does the supervisor do if the clinician continues to flounder or distrust or seems unable to learn? What about the clinician who can't seem to make it?

If the supervisor has done a good job of assessment and has been giving and getting feedback all along, nothing should come as a surprise. Nevertheless, it's hard not to feel like a failure, to wonder what else you might do for a clinician whose work is crumbling. It's difficult not to wonder how much of the problem may have come from you.

The supervisor needs to separate his or her problems from those of the clinician. Personal issues in a supervisor's life may indeed be triggered by work with clinicians and may start a chain of negative patterns that ripple down through the supervisory relationship to clients or to other supervisees. Through self-reflection or consultation with his or her own supervisor, the supervisor must trace the source of the problem.

Some supervisory relationships fail, however, simply because they got off on the wrong foot. Just as we may have a few clients with whom we never seem to be able to work effectively, personality clashes can hinder our work with clinicians. In cases in which the clinician and supervisor simply don't hit it off, the clinician should be transferred to someone else for supervision.

In some instances, a clinician has problems with the agency itself. The problem does not lie with the clinician's skills or competence or with the supervisory relationship; rather the clinician's goals and needs do not fit well with the agency's needs. Perhaps the clinician doesn't agree with the agency's focus on short-term work or its reliance on home-based services or perhaps doesn't like working with the client population that the agency serves. In these circumstances, the clinician simply needs to find an agency that better suits his or her needs.

But sometimes the clinician's clinical work is dismal despite a good relationship with the supervisor and the agency. If the problem is a lack of skill, the supervisor and administration must decide whether it is feasible and worthwhile for the agency to invest the time to train the person. Sometimes changing the clinician's work responsibilities at the agency is a good solution.

John, for example, was clearly having trouble dealing with many of the explosive, multiproblem clients in his case load. He quickly became overloaded and was unable to work through his problems. With more settled, less emotional problems and clients, however, his style was supportive and competent. After much discussion with his supervisor, he agreed to a transfer to a financial/job counseling division of the agency where he did an excellent job and thoroughly enjoyed the work. The agency needs to be flexible to maintain quality control while effectively utilizing the talents of its clinicians.

In a few cases, the clinician may be bogged down with personal problems and issues that create blocks to learning. Therapy may be all that is needed. The supervisor should continue to steer the clinician through the strategies and skills needed to handle particular cases, and the clinician's therapist can help him or her deal with the distractions and barriers that are inhibiting the clinician's work. It's a good idea to map out clear expectations, goals, and time frames for improvement.

The supervisor's greatest concern is dealing with clinicians who are resistant to supervision or are unwilling or unable to acknowledge problems; the supervisor's most difficult cases are those in which the clinician is committed to the work but can't do it, believing, nevertheless, that he or she is doing a good job. How long does the supervisor try to work with this person? Probationary time periods, productivity levels, client complaints, or other administrative markers generally provide the answer to this question. They are job-performance indicators that lead to termination. Because the director is responsible for hiring and firing, the decision doesn't fall on the supervisor alone. Nevertheless, the supervisor is responsible for closing the relationship in as healthy way as is possible. Honesty, compassion, and the golden rule are the best policies.

Fortunately, the need to take such drastic action occurs rarely. If the candidates are adequately screened during interviewing and if the supervisor does his or her part in building the relationship and supporting the clinician, most clinicians are able to utilize their talents and creativity to resolve problems that arise.

Putting it all together

To consolidate and summarize the stage-one process, it might be helpful to look at one beginning clinician's own self-evaluation. This self-evaluation was written late in stage one. The clinician had worked approximately one year at the agency and had had a couple of years of nonclinical, postgraduate experience. The evaluation covers the areas of skills and theoretical orientation, use of self, and use of supervision.

> *I tend to operate on the assumption that problems stem from difficulties individuals and families have in coping with their feelings. I am not as confident about whether my actual interventions are systems-oriented or process-oriented.*
>
> *As I begin with a client I look for pain and try to connect with each person by empathizing with those feelings. The other side of that, however, is that I sometimes move too quickly. I'm learning that one needs to tread softly, especially when looking at pain. Another assumption I carry is that the individuals within a family probably do not have effective methods of handling each other's feelings.*

This clinician does not have high anxiety. This person is able to approach feelings and deal with them—a good sign. Notice that the clinician tends to focus on generic, global issues—feelings and pain—and has some difficulty applying theory to practice—timing questions, the uncertainty about systems versus process interventions. The writing itself reflects lack of organization in its skipping from one topic to another. The passage regarding "treading softly" suggests a measure of caution and fear. As a supervisor, I wonder about the clinician's own sense of pain—whether it's being projected onto clients or whether I should tread more softly in our relationship.

> *I begin with the assumption that change is possible but that change is incredibly frightening. I often perceive the resistance as simply fear of losing the* status quo *and the familiar.*
>
> *I believe that I am careful about over- or underidentifying with one member of the family. The other side of this, however, is that I hesitate to be confrontational or to be an expert. An example is my reluctance to question why a parent failed to follow through with a previously agreed-upon plan. My fears are of not being liked.*

> *It is difficult for me to consider myself as powerful. I wonder if I let myself become more of a friend with adults. I'm afraid of hurting someone's feelings.*

Here the clinician indicates fear of change with clients and self, the "good kid" sensitivity to power, the need to be careful, difficulty with confrontation, fear of not being liked by others, of hurting or being hurt. Of course, these issues raise parallel issues of not being liked by me and sensitivity to my power. Supervision offers clinicians the opportunity to learn how to confront others, to understand that although feelings may get hurt, they can also be healed. The writing suggests self-awareness and a willingness to be open with the supervisor—another good sign for the supervisory relationship and the clinicians' ability to approach anxiety.

> *I believe that growth derives from how relationships are processed and experienced. I feel that connecting with people and attempting to allow them to experience a different kind of relationship is the essence of therapy. I try to impart a sense that I like the other person and that he or she is respected and accepted.*

Although I agree with the basic principle reflected here, I again see a certain vagueness and simplicity of belief—that feelings and relationship can cure all—as well as a sense once again of wanting to like and be liked.

> *I feel that I can be creative in my work. I am able to think of interventions that are unique to the particular client I am working with. I realize that I am reluctant to leave responsibility with those who should have it. I often jump in and rescue partly to avoid pain and to avoid my own lack of confidence. I would like to develop a feel for when it is appropriate to be myself in therapy and when it is imperative that I adopt a professional self.*

Good insight and self-disclosure here. The themes again reflect pain, performance pressure, rescuing, dividing the self into personal and professional areas.

> *One difficult area is working with adolescents' families when the parents threaten to throw the child out or are resisting allowing them to separate. My own fear in challenging the parent results in my feeling at a loss as to how to handle the situation . . . . Currently I am having considerable difficulty managing stress and have yet to find an effective way to handle the anxiety I feel at times.*

Potential issues regarding individuation and boundaries. Fear of confrontation again. The clinician is clearly aware of anxiety but not overwhelmed. Stress is a concern and could result in burnout.

> *Because of my past supervisory experience, I learned to muddle my way through alone. As a result I am in a constant dilemma in that I want help but feel unsure as to how to ask for it and use it. . . . I often experience a real sense of vulnerability, which stems from my feeling new. I often feel overwhelmed and unsure how to start. I think the experience of being given direction and feedback in the very moment it is needed would be ideal. Group supervision is difficult because it intensifies my sense of vulnerability.*

Several things here. The vulnerability, but again the awareness and disclosure of it. Also, the effect of past supervision upon the present relationship and a clear message to me to help the clinician use supervision more effectively. The comment about being overwhelmed raises a supervisory concern that I take care not to overwhelm the clinician even more. The desire for instant feedback reflects both the anxiety and concern about doing it right. The reaction to group supervision is common among clinicians at this level.

Overall, this clinician is clearly in good shape. Themes and feelings are expressed clearly, and the clinician trusts the supervisory relationship. An avoider may not be as articulate, may have difficulty pinning down the sources of anxiety, would convey an overall sense of being overwhelmed, and might be more self-deprecating. A binder would certainly be less open and more intellectual and would focus more on clients and less on self or supervision.

> *I would like to think about what I enjoy doing rather than worrying about how I am doing it.*

The last statement is important in that the clinician begins to shift away from doing therapy "right" toward doing it the way he or she feels most comfortable. The beginning of a therapeutic voice is heard. The clinician is moving away from a self-protective stance and settling into the larger work of therapy and the supervisory relationship. The clinician is moving toward the next stage of development—reflection.

CHAPTER 6

Stage 2: Reflection— The Supervisor as Guide

"Compared with last year, I feel much more settled now."

No one stays a beginner forever, and sometime between three and eighteen months after starting work, things begin to change. This clinician's statement summarizes the shift of feelings at this new stage of development. It's time for the clinician to slow down and look around, to reflect on his or her own inner process and its impact on others.

Anxiety finally begins to wane. The probationary period is over, and with it, much of the performance pressure and anxiety driven by the need to appear competent. If the supervisor has been on the ball, the clinician knows that the supervisor is aware of the quality of his or her work and has seen through the posturing and games that he or she has played in order to look good enough. It's time to drop the masks. The clinician has survived, the worst-case fear of being drummed out of the profession for incompetence has not materialized, and the supervisor has proven trustworthy.

Moving on a parallel course with the clinician, many clients are making a similar shift. Some have left therapy, of course, either because they got what they wanted or because the clinician wasn't able to move quickly enough to uncover their problems or offer the advice they were seeking. But with the clinician's increasing ability to think systemically and act a bit more flexibly, many of the newer clients are getting what they need sooner, and a few of the first batch of clients have stayed on.

Like the clinician, these longer-term clients have likely moved beyond their initial anxiety and distrust. The presenting problems that brought them to the agency are less overwhelming now. Like the clinician, they are able to look around and see the broader themes and processes that seem to connect the disparate parts of their lives. They, with the clinician's help, are able to sit back and reflect on the pain they feel as well as the sources of it.

The opportunity for reflection is the predominant quality of this stage. As both clients and clinician settle in, the clinician expends less energy on looking good or preventing collapse. The relationship between the supervisor and clinician provides a safety net for the emotional self, allowing the clinician to reflect on the past and on the self. As therapy enters the middle stages, focus may shift to a specific individual within the family or couple. The client's history now means more than just a few lines on an assessment form; it shapes the present. Sometimes the clinician leads the client into exploring the past in order to move beyond dysfunctional patterns toward the active pursuit of new life directions. Other times, clients take the lead. Usually, however, the supervisor, in an effort to help the clinician and client look beyond the chaos of the presenting problems, encourages the clinician to look deeper into the therapeutic material.

The pace of both clinical and supervisory work slows. The client and clinician now spend time looking at the linkages and dynamics of problems. This is a time for finer work, attention to detail and to the subtle emotions and behaviors that were missed during the initial crisis. The focus is less on problems and more on process.

Resistance and impasse

This shift raises new problems. Some clinicians do not welcome digging in and down. After the dust has settled on a solution to a presenting problem, they are ready to pack up and call it a day. Even if the client shows some interest in moving to a deeper level, the clinician finds reasons to back away. Some of the reasons may be practical—the agency's or insurance company's pressure to terminate or the press of the agency's waiting list. Sometimes, however, the clinician may have personal reasons for not wanting to dig deeper into clients' problems.

These clinicians are firefighters. They like the excitement of the crisis and the chance to act quickly, then move on. Pushing them toward the surface and out the door are their own limitations with regard to intimacy. The settling into long-term work feels too slow, too close; the increasing emotional responsibility makes them feel uncomfortable. For these clinicians, brief treatment is not merely an efficient way to use resources, it is a way to keep relationships at the "proper" distance.

Most clinicians, however, welcome increased intimacy. The problem issue for them is not how to find quick terminations, but rather how to deal with impasses that develop with some of their clients. After a strong start, the forward momentum of therapy suddenly stalls despite a good therapeutic relationship. Clinician and client seem to be running in place.

One reason for such impasses is the clinician's incompletely developed skill. For example, Mrs. Jones is no longer just complaining about her boyfriend; now she is wondering why she always hooks up with these no good, abusive, s-o-bs. Mr. Smith has stopped fretting about Danny's insolence and is talking about the problems in his marriage. With the development of trust in the therapeutic relationship, the client offers more and asks for more. In addition to helping Mrs. Jones contact a woman's shelter or get a restraining order on her boyfriend, the clinician must help her explore her own needs and assumptions about relationships. To help Mr. Smith, the clinician must move beyond behavior-modification exercises that tack on more quality time with Danny to uncovering the source of his resentment toward his wife or perhaps his underlying fear that he will become like his father. The clinician quickly runs out of clever tricks and pat strategies; empathic listening is no longer good enough.

But the clinician's skills generally form the smaller part of the problem; with the supervisor's help, the clinician can plan and apply the needed clinical first aid to get through the next session. Rather, therapeutic paralysis often results from the client's and clinician's stake in the relationship. Collusion lies at the heart of the impasse (Reusch, 1961), the interweaving of countertransference and transference issues, an unconscious agreement to reduce anxiety by falling into patterns that meet the emotional needs of both the clinician and client (Mueller & Kell, 1972; Taibbi, 1981).

One of the most common sources of collusion seen in all stages of development is induction into the family system. Here, the clinician takes on one of the roles within the family system or absorbs the family's emotional stance. Ellen, for example, may find herself joining with the mother and the other kids in bashing Dad for his neglect of the family; in couples therapy she may side consistently with one partner, or in individual therapy she may assume the immobility and hopelessness of a depressed client. Something in her emotional life identifies with something within the client or system, and she becomes dragged into and a part of the problem. When Ellen becomes entangled in the system in this way, she loses her emotional independence. Rather than staying outside the system as a change agent and role model for approaching anxiety, she unwittingly avoids anxiety and supports the dysfunctional patterns that are already present. She loses her therapeutic power and leverage on the system. An impasse occurs.

Impasse by seduction

During this second stage, however, the clinician is vulnerable to a particular form of collusion—using the therapeutic relationship as a refuge. In such instances, Ellen and her client make significant emotional investments in maintaining the relationship as it currently exists even when the client and clinician appear to be working and moving forward. Mrs. Jones, for example, comes in every Tuesday and recites for Ellen a summary of the week's events. She talks about her reactions, her thoughts; she sighs and cries and gets mad. Ellen may offer support or advice, even give her a homework assignment to write a letter to her deceased mother or aborted child. The assignment may or may not get done, but it really doesn't matter. Although the therapeutic content may change, the process remains the same week after week.

It's easy to see this pattern as Mrs. Jones's dependency on Ellen as a support for the chaos of her life. This in itself is not cause for concern; in fact, it is common in the middle stages of therapy. Such dependency can even be therapeutic—Mrs. Jones may have never learned to trust another woman, and her relationship with Ellen represents a reparenting opportunity. Similarly what appears like an impasse in her ability to continue to make changes in her life could represent a plateau in progress after an energetic start, a time for Mrs. Jones to consolidate her gains.

But the collusion betrays the seduction: The process has ground to a halt as a result of emotional ruts, routine, and repetition; without some anxiety within the relationship pushing the process forward, Mrs. Jones is now treading water, and Ellen is looking the other way.

Rather than approaching anxiety, both client and clinician have become avoiders—both bask in the comfort of the relationship as it is. In part, this impasse is fueled by Ellen's difficulty with confrontation, the "good kid's" inclination to be happy if the client is happy. But the impasse is also fueled by Ellen's deeper need for the relationship. Ellen has been seduced by intimacy. The closeness, dependency, openness, and trust of the client has drawn Ellen into her client's world, filling her own unmet needs. She doesn't want to risk losing this intimacy by pushing therapy forward. For clinicians who haven't had many opportunities to have their needs met through personal relationships—boyfriends, girl friends, spouses, children—this can be a particularly powerful experience. If the clinician has struggled during the past months with anxiety, distrust, failure, the sense of faking it, such intimacy can feel like validation for a job well done.

The supervisor as mentor and guide

All of these struggles with intimacy, intensity, and impasses come to the supervisor and become part of supervision. The supervisor sets the depth gauge in work with clients, clarifying the agency's expectations and boundaries regarding long- and short-term work. The supervisor, who is a clinician as well, makes decisions, in the best of all possible worlds, governed less by policy and case load and more by client needs and clinician growth.

As the clinician rounds the turn into the second stage, a certain baseline of emotional involvement has been achieved between the supervisor and clinician. If the supervisor is supervising more than one clinician at this second stage, the degree of intensity within the supervisory relationship will vary among them.

Tom, for example, may have let down his guard over the course of months and given up attempts to control the supervisory session. Although he may be more open with and dependent on the supervisor, a residue of wariness may cause him to hold back. Perhaps he just needs more time with the supervisor and in clinical practice.

Others, for example, Susan or Ellen, have reached a deeper level of trust and intimacy with the supervisor. The pseudo dependence of the first stage has given way to a real dependency on the supervisor. They have dropped their defenses and no longer feel a need to impress the supervisor. Self-initiation and clinical risk taking, resulting from increased self-confidence and trust in the supervisor, have also increased.

For a rare few, the supervisor becomes more than a good supervisor; he or she becomes a mentor to the clinician. As the supervisor becomes less threatening and more of a support, the clinician may begin to view the supervisor as a role model. What's important for the supervisor to know is that the process is largely out of his or her control. Mentors can't be assigned; they are chosen. The good supervisor remains open to the possibility; if such a relationship does develop, he or she should welcome and support the relationship as a gift.

Regardless of the level of closeness between the supervisor and clinician in stage two, the clinician must begin to assume more responsibility for personal development. With some experience under the belt, the clinician is beginning to get a sense of his or her own native talents and clinical instincts. The therapeutic world is becoming increasingly intriguing and complex.

As the clinician takes on more responsibility, the supervisor takes on less. The supervisor no longer worries about whether the clinician can actually do the job and is not as concerned about scaring the clinician off by sounding too gruff or asking too many questions. The supervisor spends less time instructing the clinician on how to plug holes in therapeutic dikes. The clinician can be counted on to get the basic tasks done and, as part of his or her self-evaluation, map out realistic and specific short- and long-range clinical and educational goals. In other words, at this stage, the supervisor becomes more of a guide than a teacher.

Turning up the heat

The supervisor can now turn up the heat and become more challenging and confrontational with the clinician. The supervisory focus shifts from the client and the client's presenting problems to the clinician–client relationship and replicating problems that occur during clinical sessions. Discussion focuses less on the broad strategies of problem solving or events during the client's week and more on the dynamics of the therapeutic relationship and events that occur during a session. Focus is on the subtle ways anxiety is shifted back and forth within the session as the clinician and client explore problems together.

The supervisor holds a magnifying glass, viewing the clinician's work from a micro rather than macro level. As the clinician works to fine tune the client's thinking and behavior, the supervisor closely tracks the process in order to help the clinician fine tune his or her own thinking and actions. The supervisor's goals are to help the clinician shift within a session between process and content, history and present, emotion and reasoning as the need arises and to perceive the client life in terms of smaller actions. The clinician needs to recognize and move among the parallel universes that run through the client, clinician, and supervisory worlds. The supervisor's job is to help the clinician see how process is really content in motion.

Susan, for example, is discussing the Williams family. The couple were initially concerned about the tantrums and defiant behavior of their nine-year-old son, Andy. It soon became clear that the parents were not united or consistent in the way they handled Andy's misbehavior. Susan appropriately zeroed in on this. Marital problems were uncovered. In fact, Mrs. Williams revealed that she had been considering leaving the marriage altogether.

Mrs. Williams asks to see Susan individually so she can sort through her ambivalent feelings. Susan agrees. Mrs. Williams flutters from topic to topic and emotion to emotion—the economic hardship of divorce, the potential effects on Andy, the reaction of her siblings and parents, her own mixed feelings of guilt, love, frustration, and fear. After three sessions, Mrs. Williams appears to be more ambivalent and confused than she was before.

As Susan describes this case, she flutters around the various issues as well. Mrs. Williams said this, said that; should she press harder or should she simply let her work it through at her own pace; should she do more intensive couple work? A few months earlier, the supervisor may have attempted to model decisiveness or help Susan clinically understand the possible sources of Mrs. Williams's ambivalence. Instead, the supervisor now focuses the process directly on Susan: "What is happening right now in the room? You too are having a hard time making a decision and following a train of thought. How are you feeling? What are you aware of right now that may be causing your indecision? What are your fears and doubts? Do they have something to do with our relationship or are they within yourself? Close your eyes and see what image appears in your mind." Discussion may lead to talking about her own performance anxiety or guilt or reaction to women like Mrs. Williams. The content really doesn't matter as long as Susan begins to move toward greater depth and clarity.

By pushing Susan to perceive her own actions and emotions, the supervisor stops the parallel process. After Susan has shifted gears, the supervisor can begin talking about the links between Susan's and the client's reactions, the actual problem and how it is represented in the process, what the supervisor just did and what Susan needs to do with the client. The supervisor might present his or her own reactions to Susan or clients like Mrs. Williams or may raise general questions regarding Susan's countertransference issues. Better yet, the supervisor might ask Susan whether she feels ambivalent or whether he or she seems to Susan to be ambivalent.

This learning becomes experiential, immediate, and often emotionally intensive for the clinician. By focusing on the process in the room, the supervisor gives the clinician emotional material to sink his or her clinical teeth into. The clinician has an emotional reference for tracking the process more closely next time with the client as well as a better understanding of the client's internal world.

Working with such intensity would have been impossible six months ago. Recall the example described in the last chapter regarding Ellen and her case of sexual abuse. The goal then was to reduce her anxiety and to get her settled down so that concrete skills and information could be taught and a plan for handling the next session developed; self-awareness was secondary. Focusing on the self when the self was so fragile might have exacerbated her anxiety, helplessness, and lack of control as well as undermined her trust in the supervisor. At this stage, focusing on self becomes both a goal and a skill; self-awareness is primary.

This focus becomes the basis for helping Ellen in her relationship with Mrs. Jones. If the supervisor suspects that Ellen is letting her client coast along because she is afraid of disturbing the intimacy of the relationship, the supervisor should raise the question of Mrs. Jones's dependency on Ellen and Ellen's reactions to it. The supervisor might then point out patterns in the process, preferably through a video- or audiotape, indicating the lack of anxiety and movement within the session, and raise the question of Ellen's own reluctance to disturb the relationship and her own needs for intimacy. Finally, the supervisor can tie the relationship/intimacy issue to the supervisory relationship, for example, exploring with Ellen her possible dependency on the supervisor. Similarly, if the clinician has failed to engage with clients because of fears of intimacy, the supervisor should confront the clinician with this emerging pattern, explore its emotional underpinnings, and model ways to connect.

By taking an active stance, the supervisor through the supervisory process isolates the source of the impasse and demonstrates ways to handle both the impasse and process with the client. By saying what is not being said, looking at the relationships both in the supervisory session and with the client, linking the relationship to the presenting problems, and highlighting the parallel issues flowing from client to clinician and clinician to supervisor, the supervisor demonstrates how to move the process forward.

Again, these techniques are not therapy for the clinician, but rather an effort to increase the clinician's awareness of the ways in which the self becomes entangled in professional practice. After the clinician is able to separate personal needs from professional goals and becomes aware of how he or she avoids anxiety within the session, the supervisor can back off and help the clinician decide what action to take next to help the client. Work performance is still the bottom line.

Dependency and dangers

Even though the clinician can handle more intense emotional content, the supervisor must be careful with pacing. Emotionally intense sessions need to be balanced with more didactic, intellectual, skill-focused sessions. The times when the supervisor takes responsibility for leading the process need to be countered by instances when the clinician initiates and controls the process. If every supervisory session becomes confrontational, the clinician will begin to retreat. The supervisor's sensitivity and concern toward the clinician should model the way in which the clinician should approach the client.

The increased energy and engagement in the supervisory sessions deepen the relationship, even when the supervisor raises questions regarding the clinician's dependency. The dependency of the clinician on the supervisor, similar to the dependency of the client on the clinician, represents a healthy step toward forming a solid foundation within the self.

This period of the supervisory process is productive. The clinician's curiosity and trust in the supervisor allow for creativity both in and out of the supervisory sessions. As a guide who points out the issues that the clinician does not see, the supervisor has the opportunity to share skills and experience with an eager audience. The clinician begins to develop a clinical voice. The supervisor feels important and needed, and the clinician feels challenged but safe.

However, these opportunities can be accompanied by potential dangers for both. At the top of the list is the supervisor's potential to be seduced by the intimacy of the relationship. Rather than stopping the parallel process, the supervisor may facilitate it, especially if he or she needs the intimacy of the supervisory relationship more than the clinician does and fails to challenge and confront the clinician. Inexperienced supervisors are particularly vulnerable to this danger. For more experienced supervisors, this problem may arise during periods of personal stress—burnout, lack of intimacy in his or her personal life, or male–female supervisory relationships with underlying sexual tension. The supervisor must be alert to these dangers. Meetings with his or her own supervisor, peer supervisors, or a personal therapist, as well as maintaining a healthy personal life, help the supervisor avoid such problems.

Other dangers stem from the clinician's state of dependency. Tom, for example, became especially involved with the younger children in some of his family cases. Not only did he enjoy working with the children in play therapy, in family sessions he tended to advocate for them with the parents. He talked continuously about the children's need for support, to have quality time with the parents, and to feel safe. He had difficulty empathizing with the parents' position and feelings.

Tom was overidentifying with the children and projecting his dependency feelings on them. Similar situations can arise with spouses, siblings, or other family members who seem to have less power and are dependent on others. The clinician's own dependency during this stage makes him or her an articulate spokesperson for a vulnerable family member's needs and emotions.

This overidentification is very different from Tom's first-stage joining with the victim against the aggressor, which may have reflected his feelings of intimidation by the supervisor. In fact, if Tom did attack the parents, the supervisor would have reason to worry that there was a problem in the supervisory relationship. But this is not the case here. Tom does not act against the parents; he merely feels more sensitive to the children. The supervisor needs to be alert to this pattern and help the clinician see how his or her feelings of vulnerability are being projected onto the child so that the clinician can assume a more balanced position.

In contrast to Tom, some clinicians may push away from nondependent, less engaging clients, discouraging those who don't want longer-term therapy or who don't connect well with the clinician. The problem is not anxiety but rising expectations. Sensing the intimacy and power that a therapeutic relationship can create, the clinician may become bored or disappointed with more independent clients who seem less engaged. The clinician may lack enthusiasm and become more reactive and/or passive in the relationship.

This is more an administrative, work-performance issue than a clinical one. The supervisor must insist that the clinician is expected to pick up cases across the board, that such attitudes undermine the clinical quality of the agency and are unfair to other staff. Agency case loads are diverse, and relationships with clients will vary. Community practice demands that one serve clients who walk through the door. If the supervisor is firm and clear, such problems are generally settled quickly.

Problems with over- or underinvolvement with clients may distort the clinical process but generally do not derail it. Burnout, however, can, and clinicians are particularly vulnerable to burnout at this stage. The overwork and stress from the first stage finally catch up to the clinician. The increased sensitivity to dependent clients, more intimate relationships, and tighter focus in sessions take their toll. Curiosity, excitement, and creativity push the clinician to do more and more while still experiencing difficulties with regard to boundaries, the need to please, and lack of skill. The clinician may begin to slow down and become less active in sessions. He or she may fall behind in paperwork, appear tired and irritable, and/or interact less with staff.

The supervisor looks for signs of burnout and raises the issue if the signs are evident. The clinician's awareness of his or her particular signals of stress are critically important to professional life and long-term survival in the profession. The supervisor must help the clinician evaluate his or her case load, suggest time away from the job, or talk about the performance pressure stirred by particular clients or the supervisor. The clinician must understand that the supervisor will take a burnout problem seriously.

Of course, the supervisor needs to practice what he or she preaches. In some agency environments, overwork and burnout are common. As the person in the middle, the supervisor may have to advocate for staff regarding agency work expectations by showing the administration that burnout affects productivity and quality of work.

Building skills

To match the challenges of this stage, the clinician must develop new skills. In addition to developing knowledge about specific problem areas such as sexual abuse, drug abuse, truancy, phobias, and the like, the clinician must learn to work within the expanded contexts of individual, couple, and play therapy as well as manage the process of longer-term work. The clinician is now able to handle more information without becoming confused, no longer comes to the supervisor overwhelmed, and is usually able to articulate the specific problem about which he or she needs information.

At this stage, the clinician is ready to move beyond the communication, structural, or behavioral theories upon which he or she has relied. Other theoretical approaches may be experimented with—cognitive approaches, Bowenian theory, existential theory, or experiential models and techniques. Psychodynamic models may fit well with the clinician's increased focus on process and history.

In contrast with the first stage, in which the supervisor often acted as a lecturer, the clinician is capable of seeking out information independently. However, the supervisor can help the clinician fine tune theory and skills to be applied to a specific clinical situation. Susan, for example, may be interested in using a sculpting technique with a particular family. Even though she has read about it, she may need help with how she might present it to the family and connect it to the session's goal. The supervisor and Susan may actually do the sculpting in a supervisory session.

Skills, after all, are best taught by doing them. Role plays, fantasy work, empty-chair work, writing exercises, together with clinical examples and stories of the supervisor, build the clinician's repertoire of techniques and skills. Listening to audiotape or viewing a videotape helps the clinician and supervisor focus on the microprocess—the mother's grimacing face, the interpretation that falls flat, the way the client always says, "Yes, but . . ." or the way the clinician turns his or her back on the father. Such learning methods bring the clinical process into the supervisory session, providing excellent opportunities to discuss skills and techniques.

Greater intimacy can be created by doing co-therapy and live supervision, which are possible now only because of the clinician's trust. Nonetheless, it can be a difficult experience for the clinician, and the supervisor and clinician need to map out in advance exactly how the session will run.

Finally, the supervisor needs to help the clinician fit skills to personal and clinical values. Such work helps the clinician develop a professional stance and voice. Questions about the underlying assumptions regarding a particular approach, the use of directive versus nondirective approaches, the impact of client history, and the need for longer-term work are viable and important avenues of discussion.

The supervisor's goal is to encourage the clinician to look deeper, to see the complexity and the consequences of particular actions, and to begin to ask larger questions about the work and art of clinical practice. The supervisor should not expect the clinician to have the answers, only the motivation and curiosity to pursue them. The supervisor should not expect the clinician to be able to integrate clinical ideas and values, but rather to move toward personal and professional integrity.

Moving in and out the other side

As a way of marking the changes that have occurred from the first stage to the second stage, let's look at the self-evaluation of the clinician presented in the last chapter. It's now one year later.

> *My theoretical orientation continues to be primarily systemic, and I see difficulties arising from the interaction of various elements. The ones I focus on include the developmental stage of the family, the family structure and economic stress, possible organic difficulties such as mental retardation or seizure disorders, family and individual histories, the interactional patterns among family members.*

What is remarkable here is not only the clinician's ideas, but the clarity of thought and detail. This is the same person who talked vaguely about pain and feelings. The knowledge base has increased; issues and problems are suddenly more complex.

> *I believe that most of the presenting problems stem from deficits in the interactions between parents and children. Parents have experienced difficulty, stemming from the inadequate parenting they received, in meeting their children's need for unconditional nurturance as well as consistent structure. My interventions usually focus on helping parents better understand their children's and their own needs and improving the communication and problem-solving skills with the family.*

Here the clinician identifies with the child, but also appreciates the experience of the parents. The clinician is becoming aware of the issues that lie beneath power and authority.

> *During the past year, I have gained new knowledge about the middle phases of treatment, including ideas about impasses*

and resistance. I have learned more about my difficulty in confronting clients as well as how my induction into the system can lead to an impasse in treatment. I am learning to use clients' reactions to me to effect change.

This is the heart of this stage. The clinician is aware of process and countertransference and no longer talks about being good or having clients like the clinician.

I often present myself as a teammate to the families I work with. Over the past year, I have been able to confront more with clients who . . . know that I am trustworthy and that I care. It would be beneficial to learn when a shift in role is necessary. I would like to work on becoming more directive with clients regarding contracts and follow through on connecting the work of various sessions.

The client's friend has now become the client's teammate. Confrontation is a problem, but some progress is being made. Confrontation with those who trust probably parallels the supervisory process. The clinician senses when she and the clients are treading water, but in order for her to be more productive I as a supervisor need to help isolate the emotional underpinnings within the clinician.

The negative side to my joining skills is my tendency to feel responsible for the family. I need to develop enough distance in order to help individuals learn how to take care of themselves as well as to help prevent my own burnout. I often feel burned out because I allow myself to become isolated and by not requesting supervision as frequently as I should.

In late stage two, the clinician is moving away from the "good kid" overresponsible approach and even beyond the need for dependency. Burnout is taking its toll, however. As supervisor, I need to do a better job confronting this issue with the clinician.

I have been able to confront my own feelings and learn in supervision by doing more role plays, live supervision, and taping of sessions. I still struggle with the development of confidence in my professional self.

The clinician perceives the experiential nature of supervision and the value of self-awareness. Self-confidence is an issue, and I probably need to provide more positive feedback.

> *I would like to find better ways to handle my anger toward clients. I am beginning to use these feelings as signals of how others might be feeling. . . . I realize now how I was more focused on obtaining approval from my supervisor. I would like to use supervision to help me gain a sense of self-approval.*

The clinician's first mention of anger. Moving away from the "good kid" stance and the dependency on the supervisor. Desire for self-definition. The clinician has turned the corner toward the third stage.

CHAPTER 7

Stage 3: Breaking Away

"I get so frustrated with these people. They don't want to work, half the time they don't even try to do what I suggest. All they do is complain about one another; they don't do anything to change what's going on. They show absolutely no sense of individual responsibility!"

Susan has just stomped her foot on the floor to underscore her point. She is mad and fed up. A lot of her clients these days have trouble taking responsibility, *doing* something instead of just talking about it. She hasn't noticed that she's complaining too and has been ignoring my own suggestions lately.

This is the same Susan who in the first few months entered supervision shaking with pages of notes and waited for me to fill her up with ideas and advice. The same Susan who just six months ago clung to my words of wisdom and believed that a close, trusting relationship with clients was the essential ingredient to initiate change. Now she talks about strategies and action plans and mobilizing anger. She not only knows what she wants, she knows what her clients should want as well. If only they would listen.

Clinician adolescence—a time for breaking away, individuating, exploring, expanding, and experimenting. The reflection and intimacy so evident in the previous stage gives way to looking outward with a greater sense of power, anger, and independence. The trust and healthy dependency of the previous stage have helped her grow. Now, with a couple of years of experience under her belt, Susan is ready to move on and away from the supervisor and begin to use the therapeutic voice that the supervisor has been talking about and nurturing all these years.

The clinician as drill sergeant

Clinician adolescence doesn't happen overnight, unlike a 13-year-old's physical adolescence with its sudden hormonal peaks accelerating changes. The adolescent period for the clinician emerges gradually. The supervisor begins to notice subtle shifts of attitude in the clinician—an increasing awareness of anger in others and in oneself, a greater willingness to confront a wider range of clients, boredom or impatience with long-term clients, seeking advice from others on the staff or through workshops that the clinician seeks out, challenging the supervisor's ideas or discounting or ignoring suggestions, increased initiative in determining what he or she wants out of supervision, preferring to work things out independently, and increased energy both in and out of clinical sessions. These signs precede the larger changes in the clinician's style.

Susan's impatience is typical of the middle period of stage three. At this stage clinical interests often move away from the process, individual, historical, and experientially-oriented therapies of the second stage (e.g., psychodynamic, cognitive, fantasy work, etc.) to more confrontational, strategic, action-oriented therapies (e.g., solution-oriented, brief, strategic, and paradoxical family therapy) or to those therapies that seem esoteric to the clinician (e.g., neurolinguistic programming, hypnosis, body work, rebirthing). The clinician has a "just do it" attitude; confrontation and individuation replace mushy talk of pain and general emoting. "John," the clinician might say, "I noticed how you just shrugged when Helen made that snide remark. How are you feeling? Maybe a bit angry? Why don't you try telling Helen how you feel?" Or "I don't know how you put up with that, Mary. If it were me, I'd be out of there in ten minutes. Have you ever thought about leaving?" Or "Billy, remember how you were saying that you're angry at your Mom for getting on your back all the time? Why don't you tell your Mom right now just how you feel and what you want her to do."

It's easy to see the potential clinical problems here. Whereas in the previous stage the clinician overidentified with children and dependent adults, now the clinician identifies with clients who have suppressed their anger and yearn to be free. The clinician may focus on adolescents like Billy and attempt to tap into their overt or covert anger toward authority. In so doing, the clinician runs the risk of joining with them against the parents. Similarly, victimized, depressed, or downtrodden clients like Mary are encouraged to quit tolerating the abuse or neglect of others and to cast aside their powerlessness.

Billy and Mary may indeed need to express how they feel to others. That's not the issue. Rather, the issue is that the clinician is moving too fast, pressing too hard to define emotions and needs that clients may be only intimating. The clinician runs the risk of advocating too strongly for the underdogs at the expense of others in the therapeutic relationship. Rather than changing the process, the clinician may merely replicate it by becoming the client's new "drill sergeant" and ignore the important issues of helping the client learn about the inner workings of his or her relationship with authority figures.

Of course, not everyone is angry, and the clinician isn't always on the warpath. Supervision includes moments of helplessness, intimacy, and talk about clients who frighten the clinician. Inconsistency, too, is part of this stage. Just when the supervisor thinks that the clinician has finally knocked down the pedestal, the clinician looks to the supervisor for advice, support, and approval. Over the course of this stage, this inconsistency gradually subsides as the clinician's newly discovered self emerges for longer periods, allowing for a measure of stability in an essentially unstable period of professional development.

Growing up

At one level, boredom drives the changes that occur during this stage. The process of reflection becomes exhausted and old, and the clinician feels the need to take action. However, beneath this boredom lies a more powerful source of change—the dying of the "good kid" image.

Our clinicians have come a long way. The "good kid" stance helped them adjust and empathize with the broad range of people and problems that showed up in their offices. The opportunities for intimacy and honesty within the clinical and supervisory relationships helped fill their deep needs for contact and trust. As they were forced to confront their own anxiety, they gradually realized, with the support of the supervisor, that risk-taking can be beneficial and that mistakes can help one grow. As they helped clients confront their demons, they had the opportunity to confront their own demons and become more self-confident. The clinician discovers anger—the door to power and individuation. Although the clinician may not know what he or she wants, the clinician knows what he or she doesn't like.

This process can be particularly powerful for clinicians who have a lot of unresolved issues from the past and little personal individuation. Recall the fantasy exercise at the beginning of chapter two. In the scene from adolescence, you are on stage arguing with your parents. What sort of argument was it? How forceful were you? Who won? How well were you able to say what you truly felt inside or ask for what you really needed? For clinicians who never had the opportunity to shed the "shoulds" in their life and let others know what they wanted and needed, this stage can be particularly powerful.

Events in a clinician's current life can also fuel this process. Getting married or the birth of a child can underscore the need for separation and increase one's sense of power and the need to establish new rules. Mid-life issues can cause one to feel that he or she deserves more out of life and that it's time to stop accommodating everyone else and assert oneself. Personal-development issues become mixed with work-related developmental issues and create periods of crisis and challenge.

Sharing a developmental issue makes the clinician look at Billy and Mary with renewed energy, makes Susan restless. The clinician projects his or her inner struggle on anyone who appears, even if slightly, to be undergoing a similar struggle. The clinician seeks to have such clients act on their issues in ways he or she only thinks about. Such overidentification, strong emotions, lingering doubts, and inexperience upset the clinician's pacing. Like an adolescent learning to drive a car, the clinician may swerve off the road, go too fast or slow, or find it difficult to know when to apply the brakes.

Using the supervisor as a backboard

In the third stage, the supervisor begins to look different to the clinician because the clinician begins to feel different about him- or herself.

The weekly supervisory session, the playing of tapes, the updating of the clinician's case load—the patterns that before felt so comforting now seem boring, annoying, and unproductive. The clinician may begin to show up late for sessions, perhaps saying that a long-distance call came in or a client session ran over. The clinician may be less apologetic.

When tapes are played, he or she may be less interested in the micro process. Although still accepting general feedback, he or she asks fewer questions about the details of the case. If the supervisor makes a comment or raises a question regarding technique, the clinician may sound defensive.

Some clinicians tend to initiate long philosophical discussions about cases during this stage of professional development—how much can this client realistically be expected to change, when should we pull the plug on treatment, when should the ultimate welfare of the kids or the safety of the wife take precedence over the parents, the marriage? The supervisor may be surprised at this apparent reversal of roles. During the first stage, the clinician idealistically lobbied that expressing emotions and caring could change the world while the supervisor shook his or her head, silently predicting the obstacles ahead. Now, however, the supervisor advocates for a little more time and trying a different tack with a client while the clinician shakes his or her head and says that it's time to face reality and call it quits with this client. During case dispositions in staff meetings a similar dynamic may occur: the clinician who used to sit quietly or second the supervisor's every comment now joins forces with other clinicians who take an opposite point of view.

Differences with regard to clinical knowledge and theories are also evident during this stage. For example, Susan, who has recently read a book on the use of Indian meditation with psychotic clients asks the supervisor what he or she thinks about this technique. Susan doesn't ask this question in order to impress her supervisor as she did in the first stage. Rather, she's trying to find out what the supervisor knows, to show the supervisor that she knows something he or she doesn't know, or to find out just how open minded her supervisor really is. If the supervisor admits to not having read the book, then Susan thinks her supervisor clearly is not keeping up. If he or she has read it but doesn't agree with it, then the supervisor is closed-minded and a stick-in-the-mud. If the supervisor has read it and agrees with it, Susan is apt to change the topic or disagree with the supervisor. In other words, the supervisor is in a no-win situation.

Questioning the supervisor's intellectual credibility and moving into areas different from the supervisor's own style represent the clinician's initial attempts to establish distance. Like adolescents, clinicians find out whether they can stand on their own clinical feet by pushing away from the supervisor–parent, using the supervisor as a backboard off which to bounce ideas.

The supervisor still maintains power on many levels, however. Regardless of efforts to develop a unique style and voice, the clinician carries part of the supervisor into work with clients as a result of the intimacy, trust, and respect established earlier in the supervisory relationship. The supervisor's administrative power within the agency continues as well. Even though the clinician is more independent, the supervisor is still responsible for maintaining quality control. Even though the supervisor may feel old fashioned when the clinician begins to talk about the latest therapeutic techniques, the supervisor is responsible for making sure that the clinician performs according to agency standards.

The good supervisor uses power cautiously during this stage. During the first few months of supervision, the supervisor approached Tom and Susan cautiously to make sure that their anxiety didn't overwhelm them. Now the supervisor does the same in order to prevent power struggles in the relationship.

This is a time for displaying tact and clarity. If the supervisor believes, for example, that Susan is pushing Billy too hard to confront his parents, that the parents aren't ready to listen, and that the therapy agenda is more Susan's than Billy's, the supervisor needs to point this out gently: "Susan, even though you did a good job preparing Billy to talk to his parents, I don't think they heard what he was saying. Watch the tape. Notice the parents' behavior, how Dad is staring off in another direction and doesn't seem to be listening." Similarly, if Susan hasn't thought through her goals, the supervisor needs to confront her: "Even if Billy needs to verbalize his anger, I'm concerned about where it might lead. Given what you've just seen on the tape and the parents' reactions in the past, what do you think will happen? Might they get fed up and throw Billy out of the house?"

The clinician needs to see the clinical consequences of his or her actions. By falling back on what works and doesn't work with clients and by using concrete evidence, such as tapes, the supervisor stays clear of potential power struggles. Overt displays of power and rank should be reserved to underscore clinically important issues, for example, if the clinician moves off in directions that are clinically dangerous, such as setting a client up for further abuse or minimizing suicidal ideation, or ethically inappropriate, such as violating confidentiality. In these instances, the supervisor must use rank to stop the behavior, point out the dangers of such an approach, and underscore the severity of the situation.

Given the outward, expanding focus of this stage, this is a good time to get the clinician involved in other activities both inside and outside the agency, for example, serving on interagency committees as an agency representative and working on research studies or personnel task forces. Such activities are good ways to utilize the clinician's emerging leadership skills and clinical competence. Group supervision is also a good option, again within or outside the agency. Group supervision gives the clinician a break from what he or she may perceive as narrow-mindedness or controlling behavior on the part of the supervisor, more collegial support, and if the group consists of clinicians with varied levels of experience, a chance to measure personal progress.

The enemy of power

This third stage is filled with its own dangers. Obewon Knobi of *Star Wars* tells Luke that he must be careful in the middle stages of his training because he is particularly susceptible to the forces of the dark side. Similarly, St. John of the Cross talks about the "dark night of the soul," and Don Juan warns Carlos about the greatest enemy of all, the "enemy of power."

The anger and power that arise during this stage can be more seductive, more potent than was intimacy in the earlier stages. Clinicians may suddenly realize that rules can be broken, that as therapists they don't merely help others to change; rather, they have the power, perhaps the responsibility, to make them change.

This new sense of possibility and power fuels the clinician's curiosity in hypnosis, neurolinguistic programming, paradoxical techniques, and other forms of therapy that seem magical and powerful. Similarly, theories that are excitingly different (e.g., neocognitive therapy and psychodrama) and clinical problems that present new challenges (e.g., obsessive-compulsive disorders or multiple personality disorder) draw the clinician's attention. The danger in becoming preoccupied with new and exciting theories is that the clinician may throw out the baby with the bath water and develop a different kind of clinical rigidity.

One clinician, for example, started working with a severely sexually abused woman with symptoms of dissociation and possible multiple personality. Suddenly most of the clients on her case load were "multiples" who needed intensive treatment that she felt she could provide. Another clinician became involved in body work, insisting that it was the treatment of choice for most of her clients.

Balance is the key here. With the first clinician, I asked her to tape the sessions so that I could study the symptoms in the clients she was seeing. During staff sessions, I asked her to play the videotape; other staff members raised the same questions I did, and she was able to learn from their reactions and recommendations. With the other clinician, I asked her to help me understand her point of view by substantiating her use of the techniques with clinical literature.

This skepticism was presented with an attitude of openness on my part, which is basically how I felt. As supervisor, my job is to raise questions and help the clinician think them through. If the clinician can satisfactorily answer these questions on the basis of clinical evidence, I can accept new approaches. If I feel I don't know enough about a therapeutic approach to supervise a case adequately, it's my responsibility to find someone who can.

Generally, the clinician independently discovers through continued experience the limits of new methods. A bigger concern is when power turns into arrogance, when power corrupts and the clinician no longer clearly perceives personal limits. In such instances, the clinician's needs are rationalized into the clinical process, and the needs of the client become secondary. At its extreme, this is the distorted sense of power that drives a clinician to abuse a client sexually. In less extreme forms, the clinician dominates the client's actions, behaviors, and thoughts. Unlike the second stage, when the clinician may have held onto a relationship because of a need for intimacy and the fear of loss, now the clinician holds onto relationships out of a need for control.

The supervisor must confront clinicians when personal needs and the heady sense of power blind them to their impact on others. To do so, however, the supervisor needs to be firmly grounded. The supervisor who is feeling burned out or unappreciated by administration, staff, clients or family, may find it difficult to maintain perspective when the clinician begins to seek distance from or criticize the supervisor's ideas. The supervisor may feel defensive and attack the clinician's ideas. Rather than allowing the clinician to roam within clearly set boundaries, the supervisor may try to reel him or her in too quickly and in the process lose the clinician's attention and respect.

Similarly, if the supervisor feels a bit stuck and ineffective in his or her own clinical work, the clinician's new theories and ideas may make the supervisor feel outdated or ineffective. Out of a sense of powerlessness, the supervisor relinquishes supervisory responsibilities.

Finally, simmering anger and resentment can cause the supervisor to overidentify with the clinician. Just as the clinician can cause clients to act out his or her anger and desire for change, the supervisor can do the same to the clinician. For example, the clinician complains about some administrative policy, and the supervisor steps out of the middle and urges the clinician to write a letter to the board of directors about it; or the clinician has a gripe about the most recent salary increase, and the supervisor encourages the clinician to complain directly to the director. The problem here isn't the supervisor telling the clinician to write a letter or allowing staff access to the director, but rather the supervisor's using the clinician as a vicarious outlet for his or her own unexpressed emotions.

Just as they do for the clinician, events within the supervisor's personal life have a way of coming together in odd combinations and coloring issues at work. When my son was about to get married, for example, I not only held tighter to my daughter for some time, but also to some of the clinicians with whom I had close relationships; I was particularly sensitive to loss in my life. Similarly, the supervisor's struggles with adolescent children at home may make him or her more lenient or tough; past regrets about separation from children or parents or former clinicians may cause the supervisor to swing too far in a particular direction. As in clinical work, the context determines the process.

Again, the supervisor's greatest weapons in the face of these dangers are honesty and clarity, first with him- or herself and second in talking openly about what is happening within the supervisory relationship. The focus in the supervisory relationship on process, which took hold in the second stage, isn't pushed aside; it's still the supervisor's responsibility to bring issues into the room and to talk about the larger patterns that the supervisor sees emerging within the clinician and the supervisory relationship: "Susan, I notice that you are confronting your clients much more easily." "You did a good job with that mother, a year ago you would have been a nervous wreck." "You're making a face at my suggestion. Are you feeling that I'm criticizing your idea?" "You seem much more impatient with these families, and with me, than you used to be." "Your agenda for our meetings is getting shorter, and this is the second week in a row that you've been late. What's going on?"

In contrast with earlier stages, the supervisor is apt to get a clear reaction and answer from the clinician; this is where the firm foundation built over past years pays off. During this time of transition, once again it is up to the supervisor to show the clinician how the process of negotiating and navigating transitions is done.

Who am I?

The transition can be more complicated and more expansive than it first seems. Looking outward can mean looking farther away. The clinician is not only wrestling power away from the supervisor, he or she is struggling to define an identity in and out of the profession.

During this stage, clinicians have a tendency to go exploring—longer-term workshops, intensive training, year-long training, and the like. Sometimes, this exploration represents a reaction to the brief, one- or two-day conferences that the clinician has attended over the years and the clinician's desire for more in-depth training in a particular area, a chance to sink teeth into substantial material. Other times, it suggests the clinician's desire to *really* know what there is to know about a certain therapeutic approach and an opportunity to spend time with a master or a guru.

Finally, exploration can be part of a larger effort to develop a fuller, more well-defined professional identity—to become a strategic or Bowenian therapist, certified clinical hypnotist, certified human relations mediator, and the like. Now that the clinician feels competent, the notion of having people outside the agency with status and clout viewing his or her work is not the unspeakable terror that it felt like earlier. Now the clinician is ready for clinical challenges.

The desire for a name and title to secure one's professional identity also sparks the clinician's interest in clinical memberships in various clinical associations and/or election to various community posts. It also creates the push for licensure. The clinician buckles up for exams, does the paperwork for a case presentation, rehearses for orals, asks the supervisor to fill out myriad forms evaluating the clinician's skills and ethics. The clinician looks ahead not only to pay increases, but perhaps the opportunity to enter private practice.

For those involved in hard-core agency work, private practice seems like the Elyssian fields—rich, green pastures of autonomy, fancy offices, motivated clients, and bigger bucks. A few graduate-school friends in private practice, who seem to be making twice as much as the clinician while working 20 hours a week, playing golf in the afternoons, and taking their kid to the zoo may make the clinician feel frustrated and envious. The clinician may fantasize about subletting an office and ordering business cards with raised lettering.

"I'll see how it goes," the clinician tells the supervisor while crossing fingers and calculating how many clients it will take before he or she can afford to quit the agency. Because agency life feels cramped and routine and the supervisor increasingly less inspiring, the clinician may view licensure and private practice as the escape hatch that he or she has been looking for.

At this point, it's difficult to determine whether the clinician is trying to get away from agency life or merely trying to move toward a new professional challenge. When I went into private practice for a brief period, I was motivated at least partly by a desire to get away from some long-term clients and to have more time at home.

But I also had less concrete reasons for wanting to get away from my agency family. Remember back to your play fantasy and that scene about leaving home. At this stage and at some level this happens again. The clinician reaches an emotional bottom line, feels unappreciated, overworked, angry, or suffocated, and wants to move on. Sometimes these feelings involve the supervisory relationship, especially if it has reached an impasse. Other times, it has more to do with the director or the behavior of sibling-staff.

The supervisor needs to explore the state of the supervisory relationship and its impact on the clinician's work life. The clinician's desire to leave may be part of larger clinical issues and patterns. Such conversations can turn out to be very fruitful or they may lead nowhere. Perhaps the clinician is simply chomping at the bit to make more money. Perhaps he or she will see things differently later.

Some clinicians actually leave the profession during this stage. In such instances, other developmental issues coincide with the clinician's emotional conflicts and push the decision along. Perhaps the clinician doesn't feel good at this kind of work or perhaps doesn't enjoy it as much as he or she expected to. Maybe the late twenties or early thirties reexamination of life choices leads to the realization that other talents and interests need to be developed. Or major life-style changes may be precipitated by changes in the clinician's personal life—divorce, marriage, geographical move, the birth of a child, burnout. Often, a clinician will leave the profession for a few years, then return with a clear sense of what he or she wants from the work.

These identity issues ripple through the supervisory relationship and affect the supervisor. It can be difficult to stand still when others around you are making major changes. Just as the supervisor can vicariously experience the clinician's anger and discontent with the agency, he or she can vicariously experience the clinician's need for life changes. During times when I've felt as though I were coasting in my life, I felt envious of clinicians striking out on new adventures and I heartily encouraged their decision to leave. When clinicians talk about the roads not taken, it's easy for the supervisor to muse upon his or her own roads not taken.

But the supervisor can also feel threatened by the clinician's leaving. The clinician is being disloyal, abandoning ship. Conversations may bog down into a heavy silence or turn into heated discussions about life values and purpose. The clinician may feel that the supervisor, an old fogy who's afraid to take chances, has turned hostile and is a hypocrite whose talk about personal dreams was just talk; the supervisor may heap on guilt, feel hurt, worry that he or she has failed in some way, and think that the clinician should tough out these times of indecision just as he or she toughed it out. For the supervisor who isn't one to quit, a clinician's leaving the agency can feel like a slap in the face.

Regardless of whether the supervisor encourages or condemns the clinician's decision, the supervisor needs to sort out his or her feelings and separate personal career and identity issues from those of the clinician. The supervisor needs to be especially careful about stumbling emotionally over areas of unfinished personal business—for example, previous mentors who seemed too indifferent or dictatorial. Reflecting on one's personal issues may be inevitable, perhaps even unsettling or painful. The good supervisor is responsible for him- or herself.

Skills—The voice of integration

By now the clinician has become an independent learner whose interests expand into new areas. The clinician has the critical thinking skills to know when and why something isn't working and the self-confidence to try new approaches and techniques. The supervisor's responsibility for educating the clinician is waning.

The time of storytelling begins. The supervisor has used stories all along—in the beginning stage as a way to transmit information without raising performance anxiety, in the second stage as a way to encourage and guide the clinician's exploration of new clinical areas. Now, storytelling becomes a way to present information and raise questions in a manner that sidesteps the power struggle. Rather than approaching the clinician head on, the supervisor gently comes around from the side.

Ellen, for example, talks about enactments that she has been doing with parents who have trouble getting their kids to mind them. In clinical sessions, she asks the parents to enforce the limits they have set, for example, making the child sit still and not run around the room.

Through encouragement and coaching she gets the parents to physically restrain the child, offer choices, set limits, and not give in.

The technique is fairly standard, and Ellen has thought it through clearly. She is more forceful now. Before, she would have been less eager to take on such difficult situations and would have spent more time with the child individually. But now her own increased sense of power pushes her to empower the parents.

The supervisor, however, is somewhat concerned. Parents with a history of being abused who react to their own fears of rage and abuse by becoming passive and accommodating with their children may certainly need to learn to set limits and may do well enough in the office. In their own home, however, without the clinician standing by to coach, they may lose control, hurt the child, and have their own worst fears confirmed. Ellen, in her impatience with the clinical situation, may not devote enough time to practicing disciplinary techniques with the parents or screen or support the parents enough or she may fail to consider their own underlying dynamics. In her enthusiasm, she may undersupervise and overprescribe this technique.

The supervisor should raise these questions directly if the concern is great enough. But the supervisor can also tell a story about a similar case in which the parents did, in fact, have trouble using physical restraint at home and lost control or about a client who really didn't understand the point of it all but went along simply to accommodate the clinician, thereby replicating the process rather than changing it. The story becomes a way for Ellen to listen and learn without feeling criticized or controlled or defensive.

The supervisor's role during this stage is to integrate, not necessarily to disseminate knowledge and information. The clinician is learning new skills but is less skilled at fitting these skills into an integrated model of clinical practice, values, ethics, and philosophy.

During the supervisory session, rhetorical questions might be raised: "Tom, I noticed you're being more confrontational with this father, but you said before that you thought the best approach with this type of person was to model a gentler approach in order to lower defenses. Why has your thinking changed?" "Susan, you said that if the client isn't willing to do what you are suggesting, he or she may not be ready for therapy. This is very different from the longer-term work you were advocating a few months ago." "Ellen, I've noticed you're not doing play therapy so readily as before with these types of kids. Why?"

The questions point out changes in the clinician's approach and force the clinician to articulate a rationale and philosophy. Now that the clinician is beyond the anxiety and the crisis-intervention approach to therapy and is bringing new and different models into practice, the supervisor can help the clinician weed out contradictions and discover the core beliefs of his or her thinking and practice.

Death and grief

Rumbling beneath the power struggles, the attempts to distance, and the clinician's struggle with identity, voice, anger, power, and loss of dependency is something larger. The clinician's needs during earlier stages and the intimacy they created in the supervisory relationship tend to wither away. Both the supervisor and clinician face a new challenge whereby they must acknowledge and mourn the change, loss, and eventually death of the relationship as it was so that it can continue.

Death, according to Don Juan, is the last enemy that the man of knowledge must face. For him, death is literal. Although, this enemy cannot, of course, be defeated, it must, says Don Juan, be acknowledged. The man of knowledge must gather the courage and wisdom that he has accumulated and face death directly.

Issues of loss and death in the supervisory relationship arise in emotional rather than literal terms, emotions easily disguised by irritation and annoyance. Its intensity varies according to the intensity of the supervisory relationship. In close, mentoring relationships, the transition and loss can be particularly difficult and deep and can stretch over a long period, as both the clinician and supervisor struggle to make the transition from dependency to peerhood. In less intimate relationships, the process will take less time.

Regardless of the level or type of relationship, the supervisor and clinician need to acknowledge their past relationship and confront their new relationship. The supervisor and clinician who see only anger and distance or who pretend that nothing has really changed impede development of the supervisory relationship. If the loss is not acknowledged, the relationship is truncated rather than transformed, and the move toward peerhood never happens.

It's easy to compare these issues with issues that occur during adolescence—for example, the parents who struggle to hold on to their child. The more the parents restrict the child, the more the adolescent pulls away. Finally, the parents, unable to acknowledge the loss and change, cut themselves off from the child and proceed to tighten their grip on the next child in line, vowing never to let this happen again.

Supervisors may do the same. One supervisor who was well respected in the community for her knowledge and skill would befriend and become a mentor for young bright clinicians new to the community. For several years she would serve as their supervisor and teacher. Then one day the relationship would crumble. The supervisor would suspect fraud—cheating on the books, siphoning off clients from the practice. The accused clinician would be shocked and outraged and quit the practice to start out on his or her own. The departed clinician would soon be replaced with a new one and the pattern would be played out again.

Freud, for all his clinical insights, did much the same with his own students and protégés, physically and emotionally cutting off those closest to him who disagreed with him. Like Freud, this supervisor could not handle loss, change, shifts in the supervisory relationship. Throwing them out was easier than acknowledging and accepting change.

The temptation to do this can be strong. The good kid who emotionally never left home now feels angry and cocky and resists giving up hard-earned power. The supervisor, who may be struggling with losses and changes in other areas of life and having difficulty acknowledging the limits of power, colludes with the clinician. The clinician is ready to run ahead and not look back; the supervisor wants to yank on the leash. Instead of saying what is, both say nothing at all.

The challenge is not in saying the right words but in feeling the right emotions. The supervisor needs to talk about change and loss. Rather than focusing on what has been lost, the supervisor needs to recognize what might be gained. The supervisor must acknowledge personal feelings and wade through this transitional time while resisting the temptation to cut the relationship off or to feel that he or she has nothing else to offer the clinician. If the relationship has been vital, differences and individuation are not endings, but simply new beginnings.

Stage-three summary

I believe that problems within a family stem from dysfunctional patterns either in the interactions of family members or between family and the environment. I tend to concentrate on helping families change their communication patterns and helping parents either to reestablish their authority or to solve their marital difficulties. More often than not, my work with families focuses on the parents.

Almost two years has passed since the clinician wrote the comments presented at the end of the last chapter. Once again, we hear a clear statement of theory. The focus has shifted, however, away from the children to the authority of the once frightening parents. Marital problems that underlie many children's problems are recognized and tackled.

Because of the anxiety that change arouses, it is not always accepted or attempted by the clients. I must remember to help the client take responsibility for his or her choice about change and realize that all clients are not ready to make the changes necessary. I am better able to recognize and help clients move beyond the protective shield of anger and withdrawal and express feelings of hurt, rejection, and sadness underneath.

These comments reflect the later phases of this stage. The clinician is now willing to let clients move at their own pace; before the clinician pressured clients to change. She has also been able to move through anger to see the emotions that lie beneath it, both in herself and in her clients. Similarly, the clinician is beginning to come to terms with the limits of her ability to change others.

I feel I have a greater sense of my own power and greater awareness of my own anger. I still have trouble at times with fathers. I feel a lot of pressure to be the expert, but I have become much better at raising my concerns and diffusing a power struggle. I worry less about their reactions.

Power and anger are the hallmarks of this stage. Notice that some of the good-kid pressures remain, but are handled in a more adult way.

Power struggles do not have to be fought; they can be diffused. Those past worries about hurt feelings and being liked have diminished.

> *A primary focus during supervision has been analyzing the way in which my personal struggles and feelings affect how I work with clients. This has been invaluable and has added to my growing sense of differentiation between myself and clients. I learn best now by doing and experimenting. I no longer feel so threatened about the possibility of making mistakes and taking risks. I am much more open to supervision than I was two years ago. I am not as intent on needing to be perfect all the time.*

The clinician speaks of struggle and differentiation on many levels, including the supervisory level. The clinician is learning independently and is very different from the person who a few years earlier wanted the supervisor in the room to tell her exactly what to do. The clinician can take risks, the good kid is withering away, self-esteem and self-confidence are growing.

> *In some respects I reexperienced the sense of calling I used to have for helping people. It is not the same as it was five years ago, but I still have that sense. The added responsibilities that I have taken on this year have helped me step back, reflect on what I know and do, and conceptualize what I believe and practice. I do not feel that overwhelming sense of burnout of the past two years. I try to find a healthier balance between my work and personal life. In the next year, I would like to do more behind-the-scenes work.*

The late phases of stage three show that the initial dreams have passed through the fire of experience and have been reshaped and updated. With greater balance, burnout is less of an issue and the clinician does not feel the need to save the world. The clinician is ready to move on to other things. Overall, she has a much clearer sense of professional identity.

This clinician has come a long way from those first hesitant anxiety-ridden steps. Many of her professional goals and the primary goals of supervision have been accomplished. Unlike the previous two stages, the boundary line between the third stage and the fourth stage is less clearly defined. The changes that follow are smaller and more gradual as the clinician steps out of the struggles of adolescence and enters peerhood.

CHAPTER 8

Stage 4: Becoming Peers—The Supervisor as Consultant

It's 8:30 A.M., and sitting across from Susan are a 180-pound girl and her 85-pound mother. The mother looks frazzled already and wears an anxious, wide-eyed look; her daughter sulks while picking some mud off the bottom of her sneaker. This is not the best way to start the day.

"How did this week go?" Susan asks.

The girl abruptly stops picking at her shoe and glares at her mother. "She won't let me go to the mall!"

Before the clinician has a chance to swallow her coffee, they're at it—the girl yelling at her mother about all the things the mother won't let her do, the mother yelling back about the kid's room, then dissolving into tears.

Susan already knows the pattern that is about to be played out. Mom will turn to jelly, which will fuel her daughter's anger even more. The daughter may walk out; at home she has hit her mother.

"Stop!" Susan yells, putting up her hand like a traffic cop. The girl actually does stop for a second. She catches her breath and is about to start again, but Susan yells "Stop" again. "I can't allow you to continue like this. Gail, tell me why you think Annie [the daughter] is so mad."

For the next 40 minutes, Susan tries to unravel their communications and emotions. Several times she has to jump in to slow Annie down; several times she has to push Gail to sound more like a mother and less like a sad little girl. With some prodding, they're actually able to work out an agreement about going to the mall and to build in some one-on-one quality time two nights during the week.

But that's not the problem, and Susan knows it. The real problem is the unresolved grief, the lingering sadness, and anger over the father's death six months ago. The mother is just beginning to come out of the fog, struggling to make the transition not only to widowhood and being a single parent, but more important, from being a confidant and defender of her daughter to being a rule-setter. Annie, sensing the power vacuum, is in danger of replacing and replicating the father's role and becoming abusive toward the mother. But there's no time to tackle these issues now. They will have to wait till next week. Maybe, she thinks, she ought to see them separately. She decides to wait and see what they look like next week and maybe bring it up in supervision.

Her next client—a 16-year-old boy who was sexually abused by an older cousin last year (why, she thinks, am I getting all these teenagers all of a sudden?), who himself is becoming sexually active and sexually demanding of his girl friend. In addition, Susan has conflicting and confused reports about him sexually approaching his 10-year-old sister, but short of anything illegal at this point. The kid comes willingly to counseling, but he doesn't talk. At best he'll answer "yes" or "no" to a question, sometimes give a two- or three-word answer. His IQ seems borderline.

In contrast with the previous session, work with this client is slow and painstaking. Susan isn't anxious about the sexual abuse itself, just not sure what her goals are. She asks him a lot of questions about his emotions, his fantasies, and his behavior. He hesitates, staring at his shoes, then grunting out a word. He seems so passive and afraid. Finally, she asks him what he is most worried about. Slowly, he tells Susan that he's afraid because of what his cousin did to him and that he will become homosexual. She asks him if that is why he's been trying so much to have sex with his girl friend, and he says "yes." Susan takes a deep breath. She is beginning to understand how he is thinking. Gently, she talks about sexual identity to clear up some of his distortions and fear, but isn't really sure what to do next. She wonders to herself if she is being abusive, considering all her questions and his passivity. She makes a mental note to bring this one to supervision.

Supervisory sessions, you find these days, vary. Sometimes they're all business—administrative and clinical; other days there's not much to talk about and Susan feels impatient. Lately, she's been saying that she doesn't have much of an agenda and would like to quit the session early. You don't mind. You even asked her if she wanted to meet every other week. Susan decided she wasn't ready to do that. More and more you find yourself running something past her for her opinion. What does she think about the proposed budget cuts? Would she be willing to set up a staff committee to come up with some PR ideas for the fall? Would she consider supervising a student next year? Susan seems complimented that you asked, and you're amazed at just how far you've both come.

Susan starts talking about Gail and Annie. She has a tape but decides she doesn't need to play it. What she wants are ideas about strategy and timing; her assessment of the process is fine. This is the first time she's presented this case, and you write notes as she talks. You agree that the underlying grief is the primary issue and whether she discusses it individually or with both of them together may not really matter as long as Susan is able to keep them from shutting each other down. But then you turn the corner and ask how she feels about working with these clients. Susan's had problems in the past with grief issues in families, pushing too hard or ignoring it all together. She herself was actually wondering the same thing. Maybe, she says, that's why she didn't steer the session toward the grief issues. She needs to think a bit longer about that.

Susan plays the tape from the session with the 16-year-old. It sounds as grueling as it felt. What do you think, she asks? You ask her to replay a section, then shake your head. You wonder out loud if the boy's sexual behavior reflects a need for nurturance, given his family and his own social development. You're concerned about the boy's passivity and wonder how he expresses his anger in general. Sex may be his only outlet for that as well. Susan nods. Listening to the tape you both wonder if he may be depressed and decide that psych testing may be a good way to help sort this all out. Susan will check into it.

After the supervisory session, Susan leaves for a luncheon meeting across town. She recently became the agency representative for an interagency committee studying duplication of children's services in the community and ways to enhance coordination. A lot of turf battles are waged, and at times the meeting can be deadly boring. But today she takes an active role and finds herself using the same basic skills (minus the yelling at everyone to stop) she used with Gail and Annie to deflect another political battle and steer the process toward something more productive. Even though she's been on the committee for only a few weeks, she feels that she's taking on a leadership role and that others respect her opinion. She feels pretty proud of herself.

Back at the office Susan has an appointment with Ed, a 42-year-old business owner in the process of getting divorced. When she first started with him, she felt a bit intimidated, but to her surprise it's been working out. He hasn't asked her how long she's been married or any of those anxiety-driven, check-you-out questions and seems to be doing what she suggests. Depression is still slowing him down, but he has avoided the workaholism that he was afraid he might get into. He comes in with the letter to his wife that Susan asked him to write and reads the letter out loud in a quiet, halting voice. She spends the session doing some empty-chair work with him to tap into some of the guilt that she thinks he is heaping on himself. A good session.

Susan's next appointment, an initial session, doesn't show. She's not surprised; the father sounded tentative on the telephone when she set it up. Susan uses the time to write up notes from the morning. A colleague, a recent graduate, asks her if she has any material on play therapy. She passes on a book and information from her files. Susan asks him how he likes the job, which sets off a 20-minute monologue—so much for getting paperwork done. Susan can tell that the worker is stressed out and knows from her own experience just how he feels. When he leaves he seems to be feeling better.

Susan's last appointment is with the parents of a hyperactive eight-year-old. The last time the whole family came in. Although she learned a lot by seeing how they interacted, she also felt a bit overwhelmed. She decided to see the parents separately while the kids were at school. Basically, she wants to get a better idea of how they provide structure for the kids. It becomes clear to her within a few minutes that they undermine each other. Susan wonders whether the eight-year-old is an easy diversion for marital problems and tells them that they appear to disagree and wonder if the kids have learned to squeeze through the cracks. They both smirk and nod their heads then point fingers and blame each other for not cooperating. During the rest of the session, she tries to help them separate their marital issues and anger from parenting issues. By the end of the session, they seem to be able to see how the two issues spill over into each other. They agree to try a homework assignment and come back next week.

Another day, another dollar. Actually, she thinks, a pretty good day.

Growing up

By this fourth stage, the worlds of the supervisor and clinician have become increasingly similar. Though they work on different levels, the clinician reflects the same independence in thought and action, flexibility in approach and technique integrated into a coherent and unique system of clinical work and personal values. The clinician has moved beyond the anxiety, dependency, anger, stubbornness, and myopia of earlier stages. The clinician knows his or her personal and clinical strengths and weaknesses and has respect for both.

Clinicians like Susan have also earned the respect of others, enjoying a reputation in the community, among clients, and fellow professionals. They are seen as good clinicians and solid professionals. Their world view has expanded; no longer just a part of the agency family, he or she has become an integral member of the extended family that makes up the community.

With the expansion comes a clarity and unique relationship to the work of the profession. Although some have left the agency to develop other parts of themselves and their lives, many of those who remain feel they are called to do exactly what they are doing, that their work represents more than a career or profession. Others moving out of the clinical stream look ahead and intuit the different paths open to them within the field as administrators, planners, and the like. Finally others have made significant changes, not in their tasks, but in the role that work plays in their lives. Those dreams from graduate school that were nurtured in the early years of clinical work have been altered. Although work still remains important and rewarding, other personal concerns have pushed it into a smaller corner of their lives.

All of them know, however, from a quick glance at their own lives, from their own knowledge of adult development, and, most important, from the lessons that their clients have graciously taught them over the years, that their lives are always open to change. Whatever happens, they appreciate what they have learned and are able to accomplish.

The journey from the early restlessness of the third stage, through the distancing and debating with the supervisor and oneself, through experimentation and grief, toward a more open and equal relationship based on self-awareness, self-acceptance, and self-definition can take years. The journey proceeds in fits and starts, even after the clinician begins to reconnect emotionally with the supervisor. Long periods of awkwardness and conflicting needs continue to arise. The fourth stage is the young-adulthood stage of relationship.

Shifting gears

In many ways, the path that the supervisory relationship now takes is more in the hands of the supervisor than it ever was before. In the other stages, the force of the clinician's own intellectual and emotional development as a clinician pushed the relationship along; the supervisor may have held the rudder, but could not control the current. Now, as the clinician's own work levels out and becomes more consistent and quality control is no longer the priority it was before, the supervisor has the power to change the boundaries within the relationship. The supervisor decides whether and how wide to open the door that will allow the clinician to move more freely within the agency hierarchy. The supervisor must decide how much power to give up.

Like the other stages, the changes that occur in stage four can create difficulties for some supervisors. For all their trust in the clinician's competence, some supervisors discover that this trust has limits. Their mandate to insure quality control gives them the license to keep the clinician on a short rein. Others fear that if they grant the clinician too much freedom, supervision will become too lax, resulting in loss of control. Still other supervisors worry that the clinician will no longer need them. They may even fear that the clinician will surpass them in clinical skill. For these supervisors, supervision has become the measure of their ego and worth. They have difficulty envisioning a relationship in which they are needed simply because they have always been there.

Many of these fears emanate, of course, from the supervisor's own personal experience—from parents, past mentors and supervisors, and truncated relationships in which changes were never acknowledged. It's hard to let others go beyond the level that you yourself have struggled to reach.

But these fears can also reflect unresolved issues within the supervisory relationship, unfilled cracks from the previous stages. If the third stage was particularly bumpy and the supervisor felt the need to pull rank on the clinician by vetoing unsound clinical decisions or always confronting the clinician who seemed to be pushing too hard on clients, wariness may linger.

Similarly, if the clinician felt that the supervisor was too controlling, directive, closed minded, or uninterested, the clinician may hold back or go elsewhere for what he or she needs. If the communication channels were never fully developed and hidden issues keep them from talking openly about needs, problems, and changes, it can be very difficult to confront these issues now. Resentment and loss may settle in and make the relationship rigid and unproductive.

The danger of the fourth stage is that it is never fully realized, that the relationship trails off into a mixture of ambivalence and avoidance. The supervisor and clinician may avoid talking about anything of substance. Or the clinician may placate the supervisor, who wishes for the dependency of the earlier stages, with thoughtful sounding questions while ignoring the answers.

In such instances, the clinician and supervisor may give up clinical work altogether. The clinician may periodically give the supervisor a list of cases that he or she is working on but talk to others about the content. The clinician turns in the right forms for the supervisor's signature or puts in requests for attending conferences, but no longer talks about the work. And the supervisor lets it go because the relationship feels stale, boring, and lifeless.

The good supervisor, however, confronts this problem in the same manner in which he or she has confronted problems in earlier stages—by approaching the anxiety. The good supervisor verbalizes what's happening in the relationship and in the room by confronting feelings within the self, the past, and the clinician. He or she talks about the staleness of the relationship and the differing needs of the clinician. He or she asks whether supervision needs to change in some basic way. Less intensive, the same, more intensive? Are there hurt feelings, old wounds, unfinished conversations? Does the clinician feel more or less independent than the supervisor thinks? Is the clinician ready for more responsibility?

In the early phases of this stage emotions lag behind the words and good intentions, and awkwardness is evident. The supervisor may offer an innocuous offhand comment, and the clinician feels criticized; the clinician doesn't follow through with the supervisor's suggestion, and the supervisor feels unappreciated; the supervisor feels finally settled into a consultant role, and suddenly the clinician is wiped out by a difficult case; the supervisor tries to help, and the clinician feels babied and resentful. It's difficult for both the clinician and supervisor to know how to support each other without being too invasive, to ask for change or more responsibility without stirring up old fears, to talk openly without fear of where the relationship will go next. Of course, it is only by doing so that the fears and anxiety are dispelled.

Stories and challenges

Shifting from the border-patrol role of the third stage to that of consultant in the fourth stage requires the supervisor to give the clinician some space by respecting strengths and differences, to offer advice but allow the clinician's competence and integrity to take over from there. In the supervisory session, the supervisor waits for the clinician to introduce the clinical problems.

Stage four provides new opportunities for storytelling by both the supervisor and clinician. The supervisor no longer tells stories because they are nonthreatening ways to present information, but rather to retell and reshape ideas. For the clinician, who is no longer filled with anxiety-driven questions, stories become a way to think out loud and talk about the work. By comparing and contrasting these stories, styles and strategies are made visible.

The inflexibility and haggling over the right or better way that characterized the previous stage give way to brainstorming and shared problem solving. Now various approaches and techniques can be considered. The clinician is clearer about a personal style and values, knows what may or may not work for him or her, and is less apt to become confused or defensive when presented with other options.

Because clinical matters consume less supervisory time and the clinician feels more comfortable at work the supervisor is able to present new challenges—a process begun in the last stage. The clinician might be asked to conduct research, develop program proposals, supervise the agency licensure or accreditation process, or represent the agency on larger and more complex community projects. The supervisor can help the clinician develop new skills—large-group decision making, grant writing, formulating policy and procedures, maneuvering within the political waters of the community, working with higher-level authorities outside the agency.

Training is another option. The clinician's strengths and advanced training in a particular area are important resources for the agency or other community agencies. Workshop and lecture opportunities provide the clinician with experience in public speaking and educational planning as well as offer recognition for attaining professional expertise.

Similarly, as can happen in states that require licensed clinicians to supervise unlicensed ones, the clinician may take on some delegated supervisory work, which would recognize the clinician's more advanced skills and encourage him or her to consolidate and articulate personal values and a preferred clinical model. Such delegation also relieves the supervisor's burden and helps the clinician begin to develop supervisory skills.

These new tasks not only expand the clinician's repertoire of skills beyond the clinical arena, diversify interests, and help prevent burnout, but they also keep the supervisory relationship from sagging into overfamiliarity and dullness. Even with these added tasks, however, the mainstay of the supervisory process is likely to remain the clinical work.

Stage-four summary

Let's return for the last time to our clinician. It's been five years since supervision at the agency began, nine years since she finished graduate school.

> *My theoretical orientation continues to be based on a family systems model. I assist the family in developing more open, direct, affirming communications; I help parents to establish a more consistent structure and to depersonalize the child's behavior and recognize its developmental nature. I believe that clients need to be motivated to change but realize that what seems like initial resistance is often just anxiety regarding the unfamiliar process of counseling itself. I believe that there is a need for both authenticity and limit-setting within the therapeutic relationship. Many behaviors I believe represent attempts to recreate scenarios from unresolved events or traumas. Generally I do not return to these emotions through history, but try to change the replication of patterns.*

Notice the shift from the previous stage. This passage has no hint of anger and impatience. The clinician has integrated limit setting and authenticity, motivation and underlying anxiety, appreciation of client history and working in the present. At this stage, clinicians can be both supportive and strong—little-kid's fears of rejection and confrontation and the adolescent's sloppy use of power have been mostly resolved.

> *I notice when anxious or stressed how I sometimes still fall back into my saving mode or react passive aggressively. But I'm much more sensitive to it, realizing that it's a signal that I need to take care of myself.*

The power of self-awareness. No self-deprecation.

> *I find myself now using supervision to help maintain my focus, to step back and receive alternative ideas. Supervision has gone beyond assuring the quality of my work to helping me expand my sense of self and professional growth.*

Supervision as consultation, as alternative ideas. Less quality control and checking up on and more enhancement of professional growth. Movement toward peerhood.

> *I would like to take a greater leadership role in the community regarding mental health and children. I also enjoyed training students and would like to continue to do so. I feel that I have much that I can teach and give.*

She's right; she does have much to give to clients, students, staff, and community. Of course, she has more to learn and new challenges to face. The transformation from knowledge to wisdom, from being good at to becoming master of takes time.

Clearly, however, this clinician has shaken those initial doubts, hesitations, and fears that once held her back. She has learned that she can learn from others and from experience that who she is and what she does are intimately connected. She has learned that the visions and dreams we hold inside can, if nurtured, come true, which perhaps is the most important lesson of all.

This concludes our trek along the developmental path. We now have a broad framework for both anticipating the changing needs of the clinician and shaping the supervisory process to meet these needs. In the next few chapters, we will look more closely at specific supervisory techniques and skills.

CHAPTER 9

Supervisory Tools and Techniques

Previous chapters have dealt with relationship and process, anticipating needs, discussing cases, teaching long- and short-term goals, changing the process as the clinician changes developmentally, all of which are necessary components of good supervision. But what does the supervisor really do when supervising? This chapter focuses on the supervisory tools and techniques to help the supervisor and clinician make the most of supervisory sessions. Let's start with the basics.

Running the session

Most supervisory sessions focus on clinical and administrative matters, generally more of the first and less of the latter, though the time of the year (e.g., licensure times, special agency projects, etc.) or stage of development (fourth stage vs. first) can cause the focus to shift. The tone of the sessions, their degree of formality, and the way the process is run (e.g., checking over the agenda at the start of the session) will depend on the supervisor's personal and professional style. I tend to be informal; others I know prefer to keep a tighter rein on the process.

Regardless of the supervisor's personal style, he or she needs to make some things clear to the clinician from the start. Most important, supervision is primarily for the clinician. This means that the clinician is primarily responsible for the agenda of the session. He or she is expected to think about and prepare for the session. This doesn't mean that every interaction has to be planned in advance—emergencies arise, or the clinician may want to sort things out after a particularly trying session. But in the normal week-to-week contact the clinician shouldn't be scribbling an agenda at the beginning of the session while waiting for the supervisor to get back from the restroom; he or she needs to spend some time thinking about what needs to be covered in the session.

Once the clinician knows what's expected, it's up to the supervisor to enforce it. Again, the purpose of acting tough is to help the clinician learn as quickly as possible to take a proactive role within supervision and with clients, to think through and articulate clinical goals and problems rather than unloading problems on the supervisor and waiting to be spoon-fed.

Of course, the supervisor can develop an agenda, which will generally vary from week to week, depending upon administrative matters. Top on the agenda, however, should be quality control, which in practical terms means having the clinician periodically run through his or her entire case load to update the supervisor's records and give an overview of the cases and progress, checking over case records and requesting to hear or see a tape of a random clinical session.

Many agency accreditation and licensing reviews require that some record be kept of supervisory sessions. A file on each clinician, including a list of his or her case load, notes about a particular case, the supervisor's clinical recommendations, and impressions of the session, helps the supervisor keep track of what's going on and avoid having to ask about a case each time the clinician brings it up. Records also provide ready information for formal evaluations.

But the real key to maintaining supervisory focus is establishing clear clinical goals. Goals help both the supervisor and clinician to establish priorities and direction. They can come from the clinician and his or her clinical needs—"I want to learn about sexual abuse, experiential techniques, to be more active in family session"—or from the supervisor—"You need to listen for themes, to learn how to talk to children, to give up some control and allow the client to take more responsibility." Goals should be mutually agreed upon, clear and specific, written, and include a time frame for achieving them. Although year-long goals derived from the yearly evaluation are standard, three- or six-month goals, especially in the first stage when so much is going on, may help both the clinician and supervisor weed through concerns, decide what's more important, and thereby reduce the clinician's anxiety and distractions.

Goals can also help the supervisor determine how much and what type of teaching is needed. Training within the supervisory session can take the form of a mini-lecture, demonstration or observation, role-play, or discussion of clinical readings. The best training is training that can be immediately applied—an assessment outline that can be used with a new case on Thursday, a sculpting technique that can be used with a couple in the afternoon. Information that isn't quickly turned into practice tends to pile up inside the clinician's head and create more confusion. Training, even case discussion, should move, particularly in the early stages, from the specific to the general and back to the specific. Clinicians tend to become overwhelmed when given too many details about this family, this mother, this child.

The clinician needs to see and think about broad principles and basic strategies—Susan doesn't need to know how to help Danny, who is hyperactive; she needs to have basic information about hyperactivity and see how it applies to her work with Danny. Similarly, Tom doesn't need to get lost in the squabble between Mr. and Mrs. Jones about washing the dishes, but needs to see the patterns of blame that keep the cycle going and understand how to break such cycles within the session process.

This teasing of themes, patterns, and general problems from the details, then applying the solutions and strategies that fit, is the basic format for discussing cases. This process helps turn an overwhelming load of 20 cases into a more manageable case load of 10 because the problems and strategies are similar; they need only to be fine tuned for a particular case. By working through this process in supervision, the clinician learns how to approach and think through particular cases. Even as the clinician continues to learn and develop skills and a knowledge base, this basic way of thinking remains, although the number of strategies, the various ways of looking at similar problems, and the clinician's flexibility to choose and apply strategies change.

Tapes—Learning to see and hear

If clinical work is the primary focus of the supervisory process, tapes, both audio and video, are the primary tools. They allow the supervisor to see and/or hear what the clinician is doing in the room with the client. This record of the clinical session not only helps pin down the process and problem so that the clinician can get unstuck, but provides the supervisor with material from which to assess skills.

Tapes are versatile and create minimal disturbance in clinical sessions. The disadvantage is that the feedback is not immediate and the clinical process is altered. The clinician, unless fairly seasoned, experiences performance pressure when being taped. The client is also likely to be wary and may even hold back or refuse to participate.

Despite these potential drawbacks, tapes provide a good record of the clinical process. Audiotapes present the language, voice, and dialogue, complete with silences and cutoffs, of the clinician and client; videotapes show the physical behavior as well. What neither shows is the internal thoughts and unexpressed emotions of the clinician and client. To make the best use of the tape as a learning tool, both parts, the internal and external, need to be brought together.

I use the following brief outline to help clinicians think about the tape that they plan to present in supervision:

I. Overview of the case: Description of the family, presenting problems, initial impressions

II. Assessment: Underlying problems, dynamics, diagnosis

III. Goals: Long- and short-range treatment goals and strategies

IV. Goals for the session: What the clinician planned to accomplish in the session and its context within the larger goals

V. Evaluation of the session process: How well the clinician did what he or she set out to do

At first glance, this outline may seem extensive and formal. Generally, it is neither. The first time the case is presented obviously takes the longest; afterward only updates are needed. However, the outline forces the clinician to listen to the tape and begin an assessment of the clinical process. The clinician can pick out sections that illustrate the process or show where communication begins to break down and thus avoid plowing through the entire tape.

Tapes offer benefits that general case discussion does not—a way of doing microanalysis of the session process, the context in which problems and techniques are played out. If Ellen, for example, decides to confront the mother, the supervisor and she can actually hear the words and voice behind the confrontation. More important, both can hear the client's immediate reaction in the response that follows and know at that moment just how effective the confrontation was. This kind of listening and gathering of information from within the process is hard to pin down without a verbal transcript. Also, it is the skill that takes the longest to develop.

The supervisor can further refine the clinician's listening and visualizing skills by asking the clinician to listen and see with a specific focus. The clinician, for example, might be asked to pick out themes of the various family members—the father's lament that life is unfair or the daughter's claim that no one listens to her—or patterns in the interactions—the way the father blames and the child always changes the subject. The clinician can gather feedback from within the process that indicates how much power he or she holds within the family, for example, who echoes the clinician's suggestions or who repeatedly turns away, interrupts, or shakes his or her head.

Finally, the supervisor can use the tape to bring together clinical thought and action. The easiest way to do this is to play a section of the tape and ask the clinician for an interpretation of what was going on, what he or she was thinking at that time in the session, and what he or she thinks and feels now. If the clinician has trouble hearing or seeing the patterns or dynamics, the supervisor can point them out—"Don't pay attention to the words; listen to the difference in the voice and watch the body posture of the husband and wife." "Everytime the father brings this up notice how the child starts to distract the mother." "You just made a good interpretation—listen to what the client says next to see if he agrees with it." "The client is saying that she doesn't know how to talk to her sister. I wonder if that is a parallel statement about you as well." "I notice you sound very different when talking to the mother from the way you sound when talking to the father. Why?" This kind of questioning helps make the clinician more sensitive to the process and to the ways broad strategies and principles become translated into concrete actions.

Of course, tapes can be used more informally, for example, playing a tape right after a tough session to help the clinician sort out any distorted perceptions of the session. As the maturing clinician's basic listening skills, knowledge, and strategies become better established, he or she is more likely to use the tape to spot check, pin down, and get a second opinion about what happened.

How much does a clinician need to tape? It depends on the goals, the skill level, the need for quality control, and the amount of time available to process the tape's content. It's useful to track intensively one or two cases at a time as part of the learning process. The clinician should tape sessions with clients who present a difficult-to-manage process, or the supervisor might ask the clinician to tape a session for general evaluation of skills. But not every session needs to be taped; what is learned through one case will carry over to the next as long as the supervisor does a good job pulling out the broader concepts.

Observation needn't be one-sided. The clinician can also learn a lot from watching or listening to a tape of the supervisor. This strategy not only helps get the supervisor off the pedestal, but shows a different approach to similar type of work. It is most useful when the supervisor can explain what he or she was thinking during the session and show what worked well and poorly.

Most agencies don't have a lot of money for extensive taping equipment. However, the equipment they do purchase should be good quality. Clinicians, particularly novices, are more than ready to blame the equipment for a crummy tape. Also, the agency should not try to share one tape recorder among 10 clinicians. Separate microphones for tape recorders are better than built-in condenser mikes, and video cameras need to be set up so that more than the client's feet or the back of the clinician's head is seen. Although the supervisor can expect some poor-quality tapes in the beginning, it should be made clear that the clinician may not get away with substandard presentations. Clinicians' problems are generally related to anxiety, not mechanical techniques, and the supervisor needs to address that issue directly.

Observation

Observation of sessions is costly in terms of time because it ties up two schedules instead of one. Nevertheless, it can be a powerful form of feedback that speeds the learning process. Like tapes, observations can be used in different ways, depending upon the skill of the clinician and the purpose of the observation.

Probably the most common observation method is use of a one-way mirror whereby the supervisor and/or other staff watch a clinician interact with clients in a session. Sometimes the supervisor watches and takes notes, then discusses the session with the clinician after it is over. Or the supervisor may watch half the session, have the clinician take a 10-minute break, provide some feedback, and then have the clinician return to the session.

Telephoning during the session or having the clinician wear a listening device allows for the most immediate feedback and direction. Some clinicians love it; others (including clients) are on edge waiting for the telephone to ring or become distracted by the supervisor's voice, get easily derailed, or feel that their power is undermined in the eyes of the client.

Instead of telephoning, some supervisors watch the session, then knock on the door and call the clinician out for a brief consultation. Although this method gives the clinician immediate feedback, it can disrupt the tone and flow of the session.

As with tapes, observation need not be restricted to just the clinician. Observing the supervisor or a more experienced staff person can be even more helpful. The clinician has a concrete model for use of techniques and skills and may have an opportunity to see the supervisor fumble and recover or find a different way to approach a particular problem or client.

The method of observation is probably less important than developing a clear understanding of both the purpose of observation and the clinician's learning style. Does the supervisor want to see how the clinician works with a particular case? Does the clinician want another assessment of a particular family or specific suggestions for working with a family member or some feedback on the interactional patterns of participants? Does the clinician work best with the immediate feedback that telephoning or an electronic bug in the ear can offer or does he or she prefer to get through a session and make adjustments later? All this needs to be worked out ahead of time so that the viewer knows what to look for, the session doesn't become merely an opportunity for the supervisor to criticize or take over for the clinician, and, most important, so the clinician gets what he or she needs.

If a one-way mirror isn't available, the clinician can bring the supervisor into the session to observe. Unfortunately, this method is not used often because everyone assumes that the client will be distracted (which doesn't happen, in my experience). Some clinicians feel as though the supervisor is breathing down their neck or will get upset about what is going on and create a scene. Such anxiety, however, generally can be overcome.

With in-session observation, the supervisor may be involved on various levels. The least active and intrusive level requires the observer to sit in the corner of the room as far away as possible from the clinician and client. This approach works best during initial appointments. The client is introduced to the observer, told that the supervisor will be sitting in for the session to observe the clinician (it helps if the client is told when the appointment is set), and asked whether he or she has any objection or questions. If the client does not object (which is usually the case), the observer takes a seat and remains silent throughout the entire session. After the session is over, the clinician and observer can discuss the process.

Sometimes the supervisor can be used as a consultant during the session. This approach is particularly helpful when the clinician and client are feeling stuck. The clinician can talk about this option with the client ahead of time so that the client has a clear idea of what to expect. The observation can be done in one of two ways. The clinician can conduct the session and the supervisor can observe, or the supervisor can be in charge of the session and the clinician can observe. In the first approach, the supervisor may occasionally provide feedback about the process, make comments to shift the direction, or remain quiet until the end of the session, then summarize what he or she has observed and make recommendations for changes to both the client and clinician. In the second option, the supervisor essentially conducts a mini-assessment throughout the entire session, then gives feedback and recommendations to the clinician and client about what should be the focus of future sessions. One benefit of this approach, in addition to providing modeling for the clinician about ways to approach the client, is having the client think about and describe the treatment thus far or the history of the problem. New material often arises.

Finally, the most involved observation is observation that essentially becomes co-therapy. Here, the supervisor and clinician must decide who has primary responsibility for the case. If the clinician is on stage one or two, it's unrealistic to expect an even division of responsibility. In the early stages, it is often useful to have the clinician serve as secondary therapist in the case taking an active role as he or she feels ready or perhaps assuming a specific role in the case, for example, taking some one-on-one sessions with one family member, then bringing the client back into the family sessions. Clinicians in the late third and fourth stages may invite the supervisor to serve as secondary therapist or as a co-therapist. Good co-therapy is like a good marriage: it requires good communication and a willingness to work together, avoid competition, and fully share responsibility.

Regardless of the method or approach, observation is most effective within the larger context of supervision. Although an occasional "I'm free Thursday afternoon and can watch your session" is fine, planned observations that fit the current supervisory goal and the clinician's developmental needs and learning style make the observation experience most effective.

Role-playing

Clinicians like role-playing. It doesn't create the anxiety that comes with tapes or observation, and they can always choose to be the client and let the supervisor have the hard part. Role-playing within the supervisory session becomes an impromptu way for the supervisor to understand what a client is like as well as an opportunity to teach specific skills and techniques that the clinician can use in the next clinical session.

Usually, role-play is easier when the clinician plays the client; he or she knows the client's behavior and speech better than the supervisor does. However, the supervisor can also assume the client role at times. In fact, the supervisor may be able to portray client responses accurately because of experience with similar clients, making it more realistic (and challenging) for the clinician.

Practically any role can be role-played—from a three-year-old mentally deficient, hyperactive child in play therapy to a cranky 90-year-old grandmother who resists therapy. Role-play doesn't require theatrical talent or a lot of preparation.

It is important that roles be clearly separated. When you are role-playing, role-play; when someone wants to stop, say, "Stop." Mixing role-play with explanations or questions—"See how I phrased that statement so that she didn't feel so blamed?" or "Why are you asking the brother that?"—can create confusion and disrupt the flow. Keeping the process moving allows the supervisor and clinician to sense what it may feel like to be the client as well as see the effects of particular techniques.

After the role-play, it is important to debrief. How does it feel to be the client? How did you feel when I was more supportive? What did you think when I didn't get angry at what you said? Did you understand why I said that? Debriefing brings the clinician back into his or her professional role, elicits important material from the experience, and pins down concrete steps the clinician can take in the next session.

Role-play should not last too long. The supervisor and clinician should understand what and why they are role-playing—to determine how to confront Ms. Thomas about neglect of her son, to initiate talk about incest with 16-year-old Theresa, to evaluate a new imagery technique in working with Mr. Williams, a grieving widower. Once the parts are assigned and role-play has begun, the supervisor must ensure that the interchange doesn't go beyond the agreed-upon focus. If the clinician (or supervisor) gets too far into the role and is no longer talking about the client, but rather about him- or herself, role-play turns into therapy. Five minutes, ten at the most, is usually enough.

The first few times that role-play is used the supervisor should check with the clinician (perhaps at the next supervisory session) whether the technique was useful for learning. Some clinicians aren't ready for it. Its experiential nature may arouse anxiety or create performance pressure. In such cases, it can be put off for a later time.

Finally, more generic role-plays are excellent ways to teach specific techniques. Susan wants to know how to use sculpting or drawings or games or genograms; the supervisor can demonstrate the technique by having her act out the part of an imaginary client. The supervisor should model not only the doing of the technique itself, but also its introduction to the client within a session. Making the transition to a new technique within the session often creates anxiety for the clinician. As with more specific role-playing, it's important to debrief after the demonstration of the technique.

Empty-chair work

Empty-chair work is a leftover from the gestalt-therapy repertoire. In many ways, it serves the same purpose as role-playing; however, instead of two people, the supervisor and clinician, playing different roles, the clinician plays both roles while the supervisor observes. Like role-playing, empty-chair work is experiential learning; by assuming both the therapist and client roles, the clinician can experience emotionally what it is like for both. But the real value of empty-chair work is helping the clinician sort out countertransference issues.

Suppose, for example, that Tom is having trouble with a particular client. He constantly feels misunderstood by Mrs. Harris or perhaps he gets so angry at the way she reacts to her daughter that he is unable to help her see other ways to respond. And perhaps the supervisor suspects that some countertransference issues are inhibiting Tom's clinical work because he is not defining a particular problem within the process, but instead talks a lot about resistance, lack of motivation, and termination. The supervisor asks Tom if he would like to try to sort out his feelings. The supervisor places an empty chair in front of Tom and asks him to imagine Mrs. Harris sitting in front of him. He asks Tom to tell Mrs. Harris about how angry he feels when she reacts to her daughter in particular ways. If Tom is unfamiliar with the technique, he is likely to feel uncomfortable and will probably try to talk about the client with the supervisor rather than getting into the role. The supervisor needs to redirect Tom into the role—"Don't tell me. Tell Mrs. Harris."

After Tom plays the role of the therapist for a while, he is likely to run out of steam. At that point the supervisor should ask him to switch chairs and pretend he's Mrs. Harris. "She heard what you said. What would she say back?" If the clinician has trouble getting started, the supervisor can summarize for Mrs. Harris what the clinician just said: "Mrs. Harris, Tom just said that he's angry and frustrated by the way you talk to your daughter and doesn't know how to help you."

The goal is to get Tom to assume a different role, using a different voice and having different emotions. Tom, as Mrs. Harris, might find himself saying, "You just don't understand how hard it is for me to handle that child." Or "This child is good for nothing, just like her father, and, damn it, I've tried everything to straighten her out!" Such responses, although never actually voiced within the clinical session, help Tom tap into the strong emotions and power and softer emotions and powerlessness underlying the client's behavior. By playing both roles, Tom articulates and experiences the split not only within the therapeutic relationship, but also within himself and within Mrs. Harris. The supervisor's goal is to close the gap between these conflicting emotions through effective communication. To do so, Tom is asked to switch chairs again and respond and to continue to switch back and forth to keep the dialogue going.

If at any time the clinician becomes stuck, the supervisor can help the process along. "Tom, it seems that Mrs. Harris doesn't understand why you've been working so hard with her—tell her why." Or "Mrs. Harris, it seems that Tom is not seeing something in your daughter that you, as her mother, are able to see. Tell him what that is." At some point, however, as the clinician begins to run out of material from actual session conversations and draws more from his or her inner responses, the process will slow down, the roles will become less polarized—Tom may talk more gently about his frustration, and Mrs. Harris less about her anger and more about her worry—and the projections will diminish.

The exercise should continue until the role-play successfully runs its course and the emotional and communication barriers are overcome. The clinician should not only be able to initiate a similar conversation with the client, but have some insight into the client's internal dynamics. The supervisor should help the clinician develop a clear outline of what to do in the next session and discuss any anticipated problems.

But the supervisor can take the exercise one step farther by exploring countertransference issues: "Tom, you've had clients like this before, but you seem particularly stuck with Mrs. Harris. I wonder what makes this client so emotionally difficult for you. Perhaps some of your own personal reactions are getting in the way. Who else could you put in that chair, who else would sound critical, whiny, and demanding like Mrs. Harris?" Usually, the clinician will hesitantly mention a parent, a spouse, or a sibling. At that point, the supervisor can establish the link and stop—"Tom, I wonder if some of your emotions relating to your mother might be affecting your reactions to Mrs. Harris"—and let Tom's awareness of the countertransference serve as a counter to it. Or the supervisor can help Tom make a deeper emotional connection—"Tom what would you say to your mother if she were sitting here now?"

The aim here is not to initiate personal therapy, but rather to increase Tom's emotional awareness of countertransference issues. Usually, the issues become clear rather quickly, and the exercise can be terminated. The supervisor might suggest that the clinician take some time and continue empty-chair work independently, talk to the family member directly about his or her feelings, or consult with a therapist. Because empty-chair work can be emotionally intensive, it's important that the supervisor repeatedly clarify the process and purpose of the work and to return repeatedly to the clinical issues at hand: "Tom, I'm not trying to do individual therapy with you; I'm just trying to help you sort out the problem you're having with Mrs. Harris. I appreciate your taking risks. Let's talk about what you can do in the next session."

The supervisor should also debrief with regard to the mechanics of the technique as well as the clinician's reaction to its usefulness as a learning technique. This may have to be done at a later time (later in the day or during the next supervisory session) to prevent the clinician from becoming emotionally overloaded. This secondary focus on the technique itself further separates the personal from the clinical, the supervisory from the therapeutic process, and the clinician from the client. The supervisor can even teach the clinician how to use the technique with clients.

The empty-chair technique works particularly well during the second stage when the clinician's trust is high and anxiety is low. It shouldn't be used at the start of the supervisory relationship because the clinician will feel that he or she is being analyzed and may tend to close up. The clinician who feels more comfortable with the technique may begin to use empty-chair work when feeling stuck, or the supervisor, after discussing clinical options, may simply say that some countertransference issues seem to be going on and it may be valuable for the clinician to do some empty-chair work to sort it out. This type of independence helps the clinician learn to be more sensitive to and responsible for his or her supervision.

Readings and training tapes

Using reading material to supplement learning is self-evident and not very complicated. The supervisor might suggest books or articles that cover a current interest or problem area with which the clinician may be having trouble. Material that includes vignettes or case transcripts are particularly helpful.

The supervisor should not use written material to replace direct teaching. One supervisor I had would reach for a book any time, it seemed, I asked a question. The problem, of course, was that he didn't know enough about many of the topics himself. The end effect was that I learned *not* to ask questions and our relationship was diminished. Both of us missed an opportunity to learn and grow through the relationship.

Training tapes refer to professionally made videotapes of treatment sessions conducted by master trainers. Such tapes bring the therapist's style and techniques alive in a way that can only be suggested in books. Training tapes can be used in the same way that clinical tapes are used—the supervisor can point out various behavioral and verbal dynamics and connect the therapist's interventions with theory. Training tapes can also be used to discuss the need for flexibility in therapy—how would the clinician have handled the same case? How is his or her style different from that of the therapist's? Do differences in style or personality affect the use of this particular approach? Such questions help the clinician avoid becoming intimidated by an expert as well as to look beyond the mimicking phase toward integration and application based upon his or her own style and values.

Written exercises

Written assignments can help the clinicians think more clearly and quickly. Having the clinician write out a summary of the three or four primary interactional patterns in a family session helps the clinician learn to look for the larger dynamics of the case. Similarly, writing a thumbnail sketch of the major themes in a client's history helps the clinician gather details into a more usable whole. The assignment pushes the clinician's thinking in new directions; the physical act of writing helps ground the thought processes.

The types of written exercises a supervisor can devise are without limit. The skill lies in knowing how the clinician's thinking needs to be shaped and developed. Generally, as the examples above suggest, written exercises that help clinicians consolidate their thoughts and pull larger themes out of myriad details are usually the most valuable. Some clinicians, however, have more specific problems—difficulty moving beyond the client's emotions, for example, and tracking down the irrational thoughts that sustain them. Listening to a tape of a session and outlining the cognitions at work can help such a clinician not only think more easily in such terms, but also apply insights during sessions. Similarly, if a clinician is having difficulty thinking metaphorically when doing play therapy, writing down the metaphors of a recorded play session will help sensitize the clinician to this type of language.

Although written assignments can be time consuming, a little goes a long way. Asking the clinician to do such an assignment a few times within a week may be enough to help him or her increase skills. As with the other techniques, the supervisor needs to experiment and discover from the clinician just how useful they are. Because most writing exercises are analytical rather than experiential, they are emotionally safe, and the supervisor can feel free to experiment.

Evaluations

Evaluations, a different form of writing exercise, unfortunately are often overlooked as an important learning tool. Part of the problem is bureaucratic, in that many personnel-evaluation forms, with their numbers and rating scales for tardiness, personal appearance, and getting along with other staff, don't lend themselves to a thorough clinical evaluation.

The other part of the problem is the awkwardness of the process itself. Too often, evaluations become the yearly ritual with the supervisor circling numbers on a form the day before it's due. He or she may attach a note asking the clinician to "look this over and see me if there are any problems." The clinician isn't much surprised by the results, and it's easier not to talk about it.

The value of a good evaluation, especially when the clinician does a self-evaluation, results from the process of having to gather and compress the details of one's clinical work into a broader, more comprehensive statement—an official State of the Professional Self. These opportunities for self-reflection become important markers on the path of professional development, providing the clinician and supervisor with a good method for comparing and contrasting change.

The process starts by creating tools that fit the needs. Usually this means pushing aside those general and clinically irrelevant personnel-evaluation forms. A few weeks before an evaluation is due, it's helpful to pass along a copy of previous self-evaluations, if any, to the clinician and ask him or her to do a current self-evaluation based upon the year's previous work. Here is one possible outline:

> *I. Assessment of Skills and Knowledge: A statement of the clinician's theoretical approach to therapy; rationale for its use in terms of personal style, values, and application to cases; assessment of specific skills and overall knowledge base, including strengths and weaknesses and changes since the most recent evaluation.*
>
> *II. Use of Self: A description of the clinician's therapeutic style, personal strengths in working with clients, types of problems or clients that pose the most problems, countertransference issues, changes since the most recent evaluation.*

III. Use of Supervision: What helps and doesn't help? A statement of learning style; assessment of the supervisory relationship and its relationship to clinical work; and changes in the needs, process, or relationship.

IV. Summary and Future Goals: A summary statement describing how the clinician has changed over the past year; recommendations for future goals, changes in various areas in the coming year, and suggestions of ways to implement them.

In addition to these areas, a separate section on administrative matters (tardiness, paperwork, etc.) or any other topic (e.g., supervisory skills, community responsibilities) that the supervisor or clinician feels is relevant can be added. The clinician is expected to write this out, again for the purpose of grounding ideas through the act of writing, but also to provide the supervisor with a permanent record of the self-evaluation. The clinician is asked to turn it in before the next supervisory session so the supervisor has a chance to read it.

The self-evaluation can give the supervisor a clear idea of just where the clinician is within the developmental process. In the early stages, the language tends to be vague, intellectual, or idealistic; in the later stages, more concrete and practical. Talk of anxiety may shift to language reflecting increased anger and power. As the clinician matures, clearer statements regarding values, style, and countertransference issues reflect the greater self-awareness and experience. By using the self-evaluation as a developmental assessment of the clinician, the supervisor can anticipate upcoming changes.

A separate session should be set aside to discuss the self-evaluation. The supervisor should ask questions about areas that seem unclear (e.g., "What do you have in mind when you say that you want to learn more about chronic illnesses and their impact?") or to stimulate further thinking ("You say that you have a hard time confronting resistant fathers—specifically what do you have trouble with?"). Often what is written and discussed is a recapitulation of what has been talked about in supervisory sessions for some time. Occasionally, though, the self-evaluation process will stimulate new ideas and awarenesses.

Of course, the self-evaluation is only one part of the evaluation process—the supervisor needs to provide input as well. The self-evaluation helps make this process easier in that the supervisor merely needs to highlight the gaps between the clinician's perceptions and his or her own. "You say that you feel incompetent when working with children who are aggressive. I'm surprised to hear you say that. In the tape we saw just last week you did a wonderful job." Or, "You say that you feel that supervision gives you the support that you need, but sometimes I get the impression that you feel overwhelmed by some of the suggestions I make or seem hesitant to say what you are really thinking." The goal of the process is to reach a consensus, to close the gap in perceptions, to isolate clinical and supervisory problems, and, most important, to arrive at clear suggestions for change.

The supervisor can't highlight change too much: "In reading your self-evaluation, I notice how much clearer and stronger you sound compared with last year." "On your last evaluation you focused mainly on your work with children; now I hear you talking about parents." "Last year you had difficulty describing your clinical style; this year you had no trouble." Statements such as these underscore the developmental process itself. Clinicians who are feeling burned out or bogged down are left with a stronger sense that, despite their current feelings, a powerful growth process is at work.

If all this clinical talk needs to be translated onto the official agency form, the supervisor can base his or her remarks on this discussion. Of course, the supervisor's written comments should not come as a surprise to the clinician. Some supervisors have the clinician fill out the form first; if the supervisor disagrees, it is discussed.

Once again, the evaluation process rather than the evaluation itself is beneficial. The process offers both the clinician and supervisor an opportunity to step back and examine what they have been doing, to decide together what works, what doesn't, and what to change.

Summary

The tools and techniques discussed here should be used to stimulate the supervisor's imagination. Just as no approach is perfect and no technique is sure for all therapists and all clients, no single, ironclad method guarantees good supervision. These tools and techniques can help the supervisor and clinician address the clinician's needs within the context of a particular case and within a specific level of development. Use them as points of departure for your own experimentation. Discover for yourself what works, what's interesting, and what keeps the supervisory and clinical process challenging and growing.

CHAPTER 10

Group Supervision

All this administrative work and a bulging case load of your own! How are you supposed to find the time to do individual supervision with six staff, all of whom are at different stages of professional development?

In the same way it's tempting to start a therapy group when the client waiting list gets out of control, a supervisor may consider group supervision when overloaded with responsibilities. Why work your magic on only one clinician at a time when you can do six in one fell swoop? In addition to saving time and energy, group supervision will allow clinicians to learn from one another, develop leadership skills and a sense of group process, find role models other than yourself, learn about different kinds of problems and clients, break down feelings of isolation, and obtain emotional support. Actually, why would you want to do it any other way?

For the same reason you don't place every client who walks through the door in a group. You have to consider the needs of the individuals involved. New staff, who are likely to feel anxious and pressured to perform, may find a group intimidating. For experienced clinicians, groups may become competitive or distracting or they may inhibit learning.

From the supervisor's point of view, group supervision may make it difficult to gauge clinician performance, quality control may be compromised, and, most important, the supervisory relationship may be significantly changed as the intensity and intimacy of individual supervisory relationships are diminished in the presence of others. This doesn't mean that group supervision isn't a good idea in particular situations; it is, if the goals of the individuals and the group are well-thought-out and fit together.

Thinking it through

What kind of group do you want to develop? The following questions can help you think the matter through:

- *What is the main purpose/focus of the group?* An obvious but important question: Is it case discussion for case management, teaching/training for students or beginners, a group of advanced clinicians, an interest group to discuss a particular model or a new approach with selected cases, a support group for clinicians working in a particular kind of practice (e.g., home-based therapy), a process-oriented group to increase individual self-awareness and understanding of group dynamics? Something else?

Your first reaction may be to lump several purposes together in one group, for example, a case discussion, support, process-oriented group for intermediate, home-based clinicians. But such creative combinations get muddy fast. Pick one goal and one purpose; that will help you begin to decide whether you need a group and who would be in it.

- *Is the group to be the primary or secondary source of supervision for the members?* My own preference is to use groups to supplement individual supervision so that the supervisory relationship doesn't become diluted. But it's conceivable, say, to have a group of experienced clinicians who use a weekly or biweekly supervision group to discuss their work and use individual supervision primarily for administrative work or support. If the members are expected to get all or most of their clinical needs met through the group, the focus and process will obviously be different.

- *Will you be the primary supervisor for both individual and group supervision?* Having someone else lead the group while you do individual supervision provides an additional role model for staff, gives experienced staff a chance for leadership and teaching, and provides an added perspective to the clinician's developing style. This works particularly well for stage-three clinicians but can be confusing for less experienced staff. Again both forms of supervision can complement each other if the group is well-planned.

The supervisor doing both individual and group supervision needs to be especially clear about the purpose of each. Problems with transition need to be anticipated as staff members who welcomed the intimacy of individual supervision suddenly find themselves thrown together in a more public arena with other staff members disclosing their questions and problems. The supervisor needs to be sensitive to the process or it can quickly bog down.

- *What is the composition of the group?* If an agency has only three clinicians, one's options for developing a group are few. However, larger questions often arise. Should the group be heterogeneous or homogeneous? Is it better to have all home-based staff together in one group or should they be mixed with outpatient and case-management staff? Is it better to put all the students and beginning staff together for training or should they be mixed with experienced staff so they can learn through their case presentations?

The answer lies in determining what combinations are possible and what the main purpose of the group is. Are you looking to create support for home-based workers who are feeling isolated and burned out, or do you need to reduce the division among jobs and develop greater staff cohesiveness? Would students and beginners, by their sheer number, quickly dominate a group and reduce the learning opportunities for more experienced staff? Would a mixed group overwhelm the students and beginners? Could the experienced staff serve as models for beginners and still get what they need?

The mixing and matching of clinicians in various stages of development is an important but not the only consideration. The supervisor must also think in terms of individual personalities and backgrounds. Who could be a good role model for Susan? Whom could Susan be a good role model for? Would Tom's fly-by-the-seat-of-your-pants approach help a particular student feel less obsessed with doing everything right? Could Ellen's gentle way with resistant parents be a useful counterpoint to your own direct, say-it-as-it-is approach? These more subtle factors can be overlooked when one considers larger issues of overall purpose and available staff. Nevertheless, such issues can make an important difference in the effectiveness of the group.

- *How large a group do you want?* Generally five to eight members is a workable number for group supervision. Other factors can create exceptions to this rule. If the group will be focusing on group process and countertransference issues, you (and the members) might prefer to have a smaller group to facilitate intimacy. Similarly, if the group is a primary source of supervision for the members and a potentially large number of cases will be presented, small groups work better. If, on the other hand, the group is primarily for training and supplemental staffing, the number of members may be restricted only by the size of the room.
- *Is the group time limited or ongoing?* Whereas an ongoing group allows members to develop an appreciation of one another's styles and strengths and gives the group the chance to develop a deep level of trust and intimacy, a time-limited student group that runs through the academic year or a six-month observation/case discussion group on reflecting teams may be needed. As in therapy, being clear about the amount of time available is an important part of setting realistic goals.
- *Are there logistical problems to consider?* A large room isn't available in the mornings, and no one wants to tie up the after-school hours that are needed for clients. Alice has a meeting at 1:00 P.M. every third and fourth Tuesday of the month. You'll have only enough time to present two cases at each meeting, and that's without presenting any tapes. It's amazing how often little factors can derail bigger projects.

How deep do you go?

After you've decided what you want to do and what you can do, you're ready to get started. Most group supervision sessions, like the typical individual supervisory session, focus on case presentations. To plan time effectively and manage the number of potential cases, some supervisors ask members to sign up for a presentation in advance. Other supervisors may take a tally at the start of the meeting, and still others will take presentations on a first-come, first-served basis.

A clear, well thought-out presentation of the case fosters clear clinical thinking and makes efficient use of the group time. Beginners, in particular, are apt to ramble through the history of the case, wasting valuable time and making it hard for other members to determine what the clinician wants help with. An outline similar to the one used for tape presentations can be used as a guide (see page 126), but it's up to the supervisor to enforce its use.

Tapes may or may not be used. The disadvantage of tapes is that they can be time consuming; their advantage, of course, is that everyone has a chance to learn by seeing or hearing the actual process. If members are not told at the start of the group that tapes are expected with a case presentation, it takes a good deal of courage for a member independently to decide to present a tape for the first time in front of a group.

How the group reacts to a tape depends on the supervisor's response to it. If the supervisor focuses primarily on what the clinician is doing wrong, group members are likely to follow suit, making the experience uncomfortable at best and generally discouraging others from presenting tapes. If the supervisor is supportive, acknowledges the risk taken, and offers constructive feedback to the clinician's questions, members are likely to do the same.

The opportunity to receive input from one's colleagues, discover new ways to assess a problem, develop creative ideas for working with individual family members, and hear empathetic stories just when the clinician feels discouraged is what separates group supervision from individual supervision. Hearing multiple ideas and approaches increases the likelihood that the clinician will find what he or she needs.

This doesn't mean that the supervisor gives up his or her role. Group supervision isn't the same as a peer-support group. The amount of clinical leadership a supervisor needs to exert will depend on the level of experience in the group. With a mix of experienced and less-experienced clinicians, the supervisor's main role may be keeping the process on track. In a more homogeneous group of less-experienced clinicians, the supervisor may wind up doing individual supervision while others watch.

Some supervisors encourage an individual approach and, even with moderately-experienced clinicians, seem to fall into the role of expert with all the answers. Supervisors who become too comfortable with this role may discourage interaction among group members and may have unresolved power issues. The advantages of group supervision can be easily undermined with this approach, and the supervisor serves as a poor role model for members. Even beginners can present their point of view, offer support, and present highlights from their own experience. If nothing else, their examples can become a basis for discussion as well as a contrasting perspective to that of the supervisor.

A mix of perspectives is only one advantage of group dynamics. Another benefit is the opportunity to step back and discuss the group process itself. Similar to individual supervision, the supervisor can use the group supervisory process to help clinicians become aware of parallel process and countertransference issues. What emerges, however, is a different set of issues. Whereas individual supervision replicates the parent–child dyad and dynamics, the group creates a larger psychological family, complete with siblings who must deal with one another as well as with the parents.

These family roles create new transference/countertransference reactions, and a different side of the clinician surfaces. The clinician, for example, who is always eager to please may be overshadowed by an older clinician in the group and become quiet and withdrawn; a quiet, anxious clinician may take one of the students under his or her wing; a more experienced clinician may openly challenge the supervisor for control of the group or serve as a spokesperson for the others; or another clinician may become the group's scapegoat.

Clinician awareness of these dynamics and their implications for clinical work represent potentially rich areas for exploration. If the supervisor is providing both individual and group supervision, some issues can be explored during individual sessions, while keeping the group focused on the clinical material. But such issues can be tackled within the group process as well. The supervisor might raise rhetorical questions: Whom do you feel closest to? Whom do you feel most competitive with? How is your role here similar to the one you assume with your clients or within your own family? How are your behavior and emotions different from how you present yourself in individual supervision?

Such questions are used often enough to increase group members' sensitivity to these issues and to initiate discussion about what is happening in the room. Taking the risk to talk about such issues within the group and connecting the process to clinical work provide a different level of learning and awareness than is possible in individual supervision. But such risk also obviously requires a higher level of trust and intimacy as well as a willingness on the part of group members to use the group process in this way.

Such trust and risk taking can occur only if group members believe that the supervisor is strong enough to protect them if the need arises. The supervisor not only needs to be the clinical resource, but must keep a close eye on the pace and depth of the process itself. The group has the potential to become a more powerful, self-generating process than that of the dyad. Without guidance and clear direction, competitive and conflicting cliques can form; the most dominant individual in the group can become the role model who is emulated or opposed; or, in the jockeying for positions and roles, someone can feel left out or ignored. The supervisor needs to be there to help everyone articulate his or her needs and reaction, to restate and reclarify goals, and keep the process on track.

The process begins with the supervisor's vision of what the group might be. Like individual supervision, group supervision starts with the supervisor clarifying and negotiating goals, expectations, and boundaries. Are cases talked about in terms of clinical options, or is it O.K. to talk about countertransference issues (the way one feels intimidated by a father or overwhelmed by a child) or personal reactions (the way one feels discouraged and depressed by the lack of progress)? To what extent should personal issues be shared—someone getting married, a recent promotion, another's long-term goals for career? Does talk about such matters help make the group more intimate, less formal, and more supportive? How does it fit with the primary goals of the group? The supervisor leads the process by bringing up topics and raising questions.

The supervisor also leads by creating a supportive environment. As with individual supervision, the goals are to reduce anxiety about the content and the group process itself, to encourage everyone to have a voice, and to help everyone feel that his or her contributions are valued. If the supervisor sets the right tone and balance, trust and intimacy will deepen, and participants will be able to take greater risks.

Training groups

Of course, the group process isn't restricted only to case discussion and tracking the process in the room. That which can be done in individual supervision can also be done, in some instances more effectively, in a group. Role-plays, for example, can be easily expanded to replicate a family or group therapy session. Demonstrations of techniques, from family sculptures to group enactments, can be realistically portrayed. Even videotaping and watching the group-supervision session itself can serve as a good follow-up to a clinical discussion of group and family roles.

Some groups, however, focus primarily on training, generally as a supplement to individual supervision. Such groups include student groups, study/reading groups on particular approaches and techniques, groups that meet regularly for observation, and the like. Training groups usually lack the intensity of group supervision, and quality control is less of a concern. The level of leadership that the supervisor needs to provide varies. In many cases, these groups function as peer groups, and the supervisor, though more experienced, is involved in the learning process. His or her primary function may be to facilitate the process.

The opportunity to participate as a peer rather than as a supervisor can be a welcomed change of pace for the supervisor as well as a chance for the staff to see the supervisor in a different light. Some training groups bring in an outside trainer or clinical facilitator, thus allowing the supervisor the freedom to present his or her own work to the group and obtain feedback from an experienced trainer. Staff members are exposed to a different level of work and are able to compare and contrast their own styles with that of the supervisor. Such groups help break down hierarchical barriers and increase staff cohesiveness.

With student groups, on the other hand, the supervisor may share leadership with another experienced staff person, but the bulk of the teaching work remains his or her responsibility. Teaching is what student groups are mainly about, even when they are billed as supervision groups. Case presentations serve as launch pads for lectures, demonstrations, and rhetorical questions. The focus is on disseminating information, applying theory to practice, and filling in the gaps in knowledge. Even though students may support one another and share their own experiences, the supervisor is clearly the expert.

Your decision to have a separate group for students depends on your answers to the questions presented earlier in the chapter. Mixing students with other staff gives them a wider exposure to experienced clinical work and helps them feel that they are part of the staff. Having to present cases to a larger group serves as a good rehearsal for the postgraduate world and is valuable in helping shape their fledgling professional selves. On the other hand, with a large number of students for whom training is a primary expectation and need, a separate group offers the opportunity to meet their developmental needs. Other ways can be found to integrate students into the staff, such as assigning them to work with staff on special projects and/or having them do co-therapy with other clinicians.

The little considerations often become the deciding factors—are they all at the agency on the same day; is a large room free? Regardless of the decision, individual supervision will also be needed to fill in gaps in learning.

Group supervision problems: Playing out roles

Finally, we must talk about problems that can arise in the group supervision process. Basically, the problems have to do with roles, transference issues of control and power, and anxiety and coping styles that show up during the various stages of individual supervision. Even if group members do not focus on roles as part of the learning process, the supervisor, like the group therapist, needs to deal with roles in order to keep the group process working effectively.

One common problem is the domination of the group by one of the members. This is the person who consumes the group's time and attention by always presenting his or her cases and opinions. How this domination is handled depends on the goals of the group as well as other underlying issues. If the person always feels frantic about his or her cases, the supervisor needs to take a closer look at what is occurring during individual supervision, within the supervisory relationship, and in his or her assessment of the clinician. A new clinician who still feels intimidated in individual supervision may lean more heavily on the group for advice because the group environment feels safer and the relationships less threatening. Or the supervisor may learn how the clinician handles anxiety by trying to gather as much information from other staff as possible or realize that the clinician's knowledge base is much smaller than he or she thought. If the supervisor suspects that any of these is the real problem, he or she needs to raise the issue in individual supervision.

But sometimes domination reflects the clinician's jockeying for control and power within the group. If the group is a long-term, ongoing group with a focus on group process, the supervisor may choose to let the clinician run full course and see how the group members handle it; the supervisor may simply point out the process in order to give members permission to tackle it.

The supervisor also needs to determine whether the individual's domination truly impedes participation of other members or whether it is primarily a threat to the supervisor. As in group or family therapy, a co-leader often emerges as the group process unfolds. This person can be an additional support and role model for others, and his or her leadership can represent a further step in the clinician's own development. But if the supervisor lacks confidence in his or her own role and skills, such challenges can be viewed as a threat.

The supervisor must sort out whether the problem lies with the group member or him- or herself. Bringing the issue to one's own supervisor or having a colleague observe the group or a tape of a group session can raise questions that the supervisor is afraid to ask.

If the supervisor decides that the emerging co-leader is genuinely undermining both the supervisor's leadership and the group process and that the group does not have the resources or the time to handle this issue, the supervisor will need to take decisive action. One pattern to be particularly alert to is the third-stage clinician's power struggle with the supervisor in a group composed of less-experienced staff. The danger here is replication of family dynamics whereby the weaker parent (the clinician) joins with the children (the other group members) against the more dominant parent (the supervisor). The group members may become swept into the conflict as the clinician and supervisor battle it out. Again, making everyone aware of the process that is occurring is an important learning tool, but the process must be stopped quickly. If it continues for too long, the group's purpose will be sabotaged.

The better approach is to separate the relationship issues during individual supervision by discussing the group, the relationship, and problems with the clinician. This is usually enough to reduce the intensity of the relationship. The other way to handle the problem is to bring it up in the group itself. This approach can be especially useful if the group is designed to focus on such issues and if other members are experienced enough and feel safe enough to participate in the discussion. However, if the group consists primarily of new clinicians who are anxious about their own cases or intimidated by more experienced clinicians, members may not have the emotional resources and knowledge to analyze the process. In that case, the clinician and supervisor should work it out on their own.

The flip side to the domineering clinician is the quiet, lost-child member of the group. Sometimes the problem works itself out over time as the clinician begins to feel safe with the other members. Gently and supportively pointing out the person's behavior may be enough to stir him or her into a more assertive role. If the person remains quiet too long and always appears to be confused about what he or she thinks, the supervisor should reassess whether the group is appropriate for the clinician's needs. The clinician may need to stay with individual supervision until he or she becomes more confident and less anxious. Or the supervisor may need to determine whether personal issues are being activated by the group process that the clinician needs to sort out. These issues can be discussed during individual supervision.

The good supervisor never tolerates scapegoating during group sessions. Fortunately, scapegoating rarely occurs because group members are usually well-mannered and sensitive to such issues. However, more subtle discounting of and disregard for a group member sometimes occurs, for example, when someone rolls his or her eyes or smirks—and others respond, though quietly, in agreement—when a particular member starts to speak.

The supervisor needs to be careful not to support such behaviors out of a need to feel part of the group or because of anxiety about raising the issue—again, the supervisor has the leadership responsibility to approach anxiety.

But stopping scapegoating is not the same as finding the cause. There may be personality issues that are being played out within the group process that need to be examined by the group as a whole. Or clinical issues may be a concern: Does the clinician need help in a particular area? Is he or she seen as less than competent by the other group members because he or she really lacks expertise? The supervisor must handle such issues through individual supervision.

Summary

The dynamics of group supervision are a variation of the larger dynamics of clinical supervision. The themes that emerge when we talk about group problems and group process are the same themes we have emphasized throughout our discussion of the supervisory process: the need to talk about problems and process, to begin with a clear vision of what is possible, to take into account the differing needs of clinicians at varying stages of professional development. The supervisor's skills in group supervision can and will develop with increased experience with group dynamics. To develop a group supervision style, the supervisor needs to do what he or she has been doing all along—approach anxiety, trust his or her foundation of skills, and be willing to make mistakes and learn from them.

CHAPTER 11

Supervision of Supervision

Supervision of supervision—you can almost image a pair of eyes peering over your shoulder as you peer over the shoulder of a clinician. And in its way, the image is accurate—another level is added to the hierarchy of responsibility and quality control. The supervisor must not only check the work of clinicians, but novice supervisors and the clinicians under them as well.

Supervision of supervision, the same word tripping over itself, reflects the awkwardness of the situation. The experienced clinician, who doesn't feel like a novice, suddenly becomes a novice again, but usually somewhat reluctantly. No one likes to step back, especially just as the supervisory relationship had finally leveled out, just when the supervisor and clinician were almost peers. There's a feeling of starting over. Why can't the supervisor just go ahead and assign you some staff to supervise, help you with questions as they arise, and leave it at that.

But supervision isn't a higher-octane form of therapy. Supervision is more than a bump up in the organizational chart; it requires a separate set of skills and a different way of thinking, both of which need to be taught and learned. Just as being a good clinician doesn't mean that one will be a good supervisor, being a good supervisor doesn't mean that one will be a good trainer of supervisors.

Many clinicians don't want to be a supervisor. From their perspective, supervision seems to be too political and too administrative. They enjoy the one-on-one contact with clients, like to flex their clinical muscles, appreciate the creativity and flexibility that they (mistakenly) assume is diluted in supervision. They feel their calling is clinical work.

But many others do want to take that next step, especially those who stay with agency work. In addition to more money and higher status, supervision may appear to be the logical next step for the clinician who is feeling restless or bored with clinical work. Also, the clinician who has had a good relationship with his or her supervisor is likely to perceive the value of supervision and wish to pass what he or she has received on to others.

Making the shift

On the surface, supervision may appear to be a snap to the clinician. Even though supervision isn't exactly the same as therapy, the skills fall within the same family of skills—working with people. The clinician who knows how to help clients should be able to help other clinicians.

Of course, the clinician is partially correct. The skills of clinical work do carry over into supervision. However, the knowledge connected to clinical skills and goals changes. Although the supervisor teaches, assesses, supports, and challenges the clinician, he or she does so by using new information for new purposes. The supervisor facilitates a fellow clinician's professional development in order to ensure quality within the agency, whereas the clinician facilitates client growth in order to ensure emotional health.

The new supervisor must integrate new knowledge and skills into a new context, develop a supervisory style as unique and powerful as his or her clinical style. The shifting of gears can stir new anxieties. Like the new clinician, the new supervisor feels the pressures to perform and learn new skills. And the supervisor of the supervisor faces the anxiety of revealing and possibly losing part of a power base. He or she may stumble in trying to articulate ideas about the supervisory process, which may be less well-shaped within his or her mind, and fall back on remote therapy, focusing on client issues rather than clinician issues. Nevertheless, the new supervisor needs information on how to challenge and develop the clinicians whom he or she supervises.

The good supervisor understands that it is his or her responsibility to set the pace, approach the anxiety, and articulate the life of the supervisor. He or she must remain focused on the new supervisor in the room, rather than the client down the hall, and make sure that the new supervisor does the same.

Starting over

A good way to encourage this shift is to set aside a separate session with the new supervisor during which the focus is on supervision, not on clinical work. During these sessions the supervisor should make sure that the clinician doesn't slip in "quick" questions about clinical cases or distract the session work with idle chit-chat or office gossip. The supervisor needs to lay out clear expectations about the process—how supervisory cases will be presented, whether taping is expected, and so forth.

In this new relationship, the developmental tasks so well mastered in clinical work rise up again. The clinician is once again a beginner who feels anxious about taping, worried about how well things are going and what the supervisor thinks. The new supervisor may stumble and become confused. Eventually, however, things will settle down. The clinician will begin to feel comfortable with the dynamics of this new relationship and perceive the supervisor as a source of advice and information. The recently promoted clinician will begin to find his or her own supervisory voice.

This new supervisory relationship is both similar to and different from the old one. The new supervisor has a more solid personal and professional foundation from which to draw strength and by which to integrate new information than does the new clinician. Unlike the beginning clinician, the experienced clinician has a better grasp on what makes him or her tick and has developed over the years a wider range of personal and professional resources upon which to draw.

Of course, one of these resources is the past supervisory relationship itself. The trust and intimacy are already there, even when the anxiety pulls the clinician back. The new relationship may elicit feelings of *déjà vu,* which, too, become grist for the supervisory mill. As the clinician becomes aware of the developmental processes of his or her supervisees, the supervisor is able to draw a parallel with what is occurring in the new supervisor's own development there in the room.

The supervisor needs to make the clinician aware of the parallels between the old and new relationships and processes to clarify and define the emerging themes, obstacles, and goals. Although the content of the conversation may change, the subject—growth and mastery—is the same.

The supervisor once again tells stories, drawing from the history of their relationship: "Remember when you came to me troubled about your first case with young children?" "Remember how you felt when I put you in charge of the group?" "Remember how upset I was when you refused to see that father in jail?" "Remember when" stories recast the clinician's history from the supervisor's perspective as well as illustrate the supervisor's own struggle to set priorities and join knowledge with skills. Because such stories stir memories and feelings, they help the new supervisor empathize with his or her supervisees. In fact, they often become templates according to which the new supervisor conducts supervision.

Entering supervision of supervision with a clinician with whom the supervisor has worked for a long time is the ideal situation, but not necessarily the most common. Sometimes agencies hire an experienced clinician from the outside as a supervisor, or perhaps someone from within the agency with whom the new supervisor hasn't worked may be asked to supervise a new supervisor. In these cases, the developmental process can be more strenuous for both individuals. The relationship is starting from scratch; trust and intimacy are lacking.

In their absence the clinician carries into the relationship the emotional baggage and expectations from previous supervisory relationships. In addition to worrying about being supervised by a relative stranger, the new supervisor may feel self-conscious about his or her clinical skills. New supervisors may feel that the training supervisor will discover that they not only can't do supervision, they can't do therapy either. These irrational emotions and fears obviously can bog down the relationship and the developmental process.

With this in mind, the supervisor needs to enter the relationship carefully and gently, take the time to assess the new supervisor's skills, set clear goals, talk about expectations and past supervisory relationships, and give the new supervisor a chance to get to know the supervisor and feel comfortable with his or her style. The new supervisor moves at a faster pace than does the novice clinician because the resources and skills are there to push the process along. The supervisor merely needs to discover the gaps in the relationship—where the anxiety lies and where growth needs to be fostered.

Learning skills

Although the basic learning process is the same, the clinician needs to acquire the information and learn the skills that differentiate supervision from clinical work. He or she can take a course at the university, enroll in a management-training seminar, or look for a supervision group in the community. Such resources can provide a good start. When these opportunities aren't easily available, the clinician should do a lot of reading and apply with the help of the supervisor the knowledge he or she acquires on the job.

What supervisory approach should the supervisor teach? The natural inclination is to teach what the supervisor knows. In theory this sounds fine, but the style of a supervisor who has many years of experience may be eclectic and difficult to teach. The supervisor can lead the clinician toward a particular supervisory orientation—a systems, object-relations, problem-solving, or communication-based approach. The values, assumptions, ways of approaching people, and problems of such approaches are grounded within a well-established clinical school or perspective.

Ideally, the teaching orientation should match the style and values of both the supervisor and clinician. Their styles, however, may not be the same. Even though the supervisor, for example, may see him- or herself primarily as a systems-oriented clinician and supervisor, the clinician may feel more comfortable with psychomotor or psychodynamic approaches. Although this sharing of strengths may have served the agency and earlier supervisory relationship well, vast differences in clinical philosophies and core assumptions can pose problems when the supervision of supervision begins. Therefore, the supervisor and clinician should make sure that they can both comfortably agree upon and work within the model they choose.

Books on clinical supervision, such as this one, can help the clinician begin to think like a supervisor, to become intellectually sensitive to patterns, options, and common problems. But like clinical development, supervisory ideas become grounded when they are witnessed firsthand. Having the clinician observe supervisory sessions, attend supervisory meetings, and watch tapes provide the clinician with a live model and help orient him or her to the role.

Training revolves around the clinician's supervisory sessions with his or her own supervisees. Taping can be used in exactly the same way that it is used with clinical sessions, with the goals to help the clinician hear the patterns in the supervisee's clinical work; to detect the supervisee's and clinician's countertransference issues; to become sensitive to the parallel process; to learn how to assess skills, evaluate progress, and use the relationship to maximize professional growth.

The supervisor assesses the clinician's behavior to determine how his or her relationships with and training of supervisees are progressing. Is the clinician too confrontational and too demanding of his or her supervisees? Are supervisory sessions without structure? Does the clinician focus too much on the supervisee's clients rather than on the supervisee's performance? How do these issues affect the clinician's view of the supervisor? Once again, the supervisor is at the head of the chain; the parallel process starts and ends there.

All the adjunct techniques that were used in clinical supervision can be applied in supervision of supervision—empty-chair work to isolate the clinician's countertransference issues with the supervisee, role-playing, demonstration of techniques, live supervision of supervision, observation through one-way mirrors, and the like. Large agencies may even have group supervision of supervision. Although the techniques are familiar, the supervisor needs to clarify repeatedly the ways in which supervision is different from clinical work in order to draw lines between personal growth, professional development, and quality control.

Welcome to administration

Responsibility for quality control is the new hat the clinician must wear, and administration is the other side of the supervisory process that the clinician needs to learn. A lot of this, of course, is bureaucratic trivia—orienting staff to new forms, letting staff know about budget concerns, urging everyone to show up at the fund-raising softball game or a city council meeting. Although such concerns have little to do with clinical practice, the responsibility for quality control, personnel evaluation, hiring, and firing does.

This shift may be difficult for the new supervisor to make. Responsibility in the clinical relationship is often shared by the clinician and client. The client as consumer may ultimately decide how far the process will go and how things will turn out. As supervisor, however, the clinician's sense of hierarchy and responsibility are more clearly defined—the clinical buck stops at his or her desk. This can take some getting used to, especially for clinicians whose clinical style and relationships tend to be warm and nurturing. Assuming power becomes even more difficult for the clinician who is feeling shaky about his or her supervisory skills. If things don't work out in therapy, the client can pull out and find another therapist. If things don't work out on a job, an individual may be fired and a career derailed.

While being empathetic to the clinician's feelings, the supervisor needs to be clear about what the clinician's responsibilities as supervisor are. He or she needs to support the clinician's power to make decisions and resist the temptation to use the clinician as a conduit for his or her own quality control of the clinician's supervisees.

With power comes politics, an aspect of the agency environment that may be new to the clinician. The clinician is pulled into a new world—money, business, influence—and has to work with new, nonclinical people on the staff—the director, other supervisors, personnel directors. The supervisor must help the clinician learn to navigate these waters by advising how to become sensitive to political issues and teaching the language and skills needed to work with nonclinical people in political situations.

Moving up and out

The clinician who moves into supervision leaves behind the familiar roles and the supportive relationships with clinical staff. He or she eventually must come to grips with the isolation and awkwardness of being in the middle. For some, this can be harder than handling power. The new supervisor may feel lonely and miss being part of the clinical staff sibling group. They have suffered a loss; until they can find a new place in the middle and feel confident about their new role, they need support.

The transition is made even more difficult by the reactions of clinical staff. Being plucked out of the sibling group to assume a higher position on the hierarchical ladder disrupts the system. If the clinician has much more experience and seniority than the other clinicians, this disruption may be minimal. But the situation can be awkward for others. In fact, one or two clinical staff persons may decide that it's time to move on to private practice or another agency following the promotion of a peer.

Such developments can stir up guilt in the clinician, which in turn can create performance pressure and a sense of isolation. Supervising a clinician who just a few days ago was a peer can be particularly awkward.

Such situations should be avoided if it's possible to do so. It's too difficult and usually inappropriate to try to supervise friends. The roles become too confused, and the supervisory relationship flounders. The clinician is better off supervising students, new staff, or staff in lower-level positions or on different teams.

Even with the supervisor's help in making this transition and the clinician's awareness that awkwardness is normal, some new supervisors decide to pull out after a short period. The job isn't what they thought it would be; they would rather stay in the clinical trenches doing what they know and like best and where they can feel a part of the larger team. In such instances, the supervisor of the supervisor shouldn't feel guilty or that he or she hasn't done a good job; it's all part of the developmental process.

Discovering new visions

The long-range goal of the supervisor, of course, is not only to pass on skills and help the clinician feel comfortable and competent as a supervisor, but to help the clinician develop a supervisory style and voice. Usually the process flows from the bottom up, and the clinician's supervisory style will closely resemble his or her clinical style. But not in all cases. Sometimes the shift in perspective, power, and responsibility opens new doors of emotions and perceptions within the clinician. Basic values, beliefs, and assumptions may be reexamined. Instead of the supervisory style reflecting the clinical one, the clinical stance grows to match the new supervisory style.

The impact of the learning process ripples through the supervisory relationship as well. The new level of involvement and collaboration cuts deeper pathways of intimacy and shared history into close, long-standing supervisory relationships. Or the new relationship may stretch the relationship beyond its limits, causing the supervisory relationship to collapse. Old unresolved issues may resurface as a result of reaching the limits of intimacy—similar to the way some long marriages suddenly collapse after the kids leave home and the couple is forced to confront new developmental tasks.

But if the foundation of communication and trust is strong, the supervisor and clinician have the opportunity to acknowledge their indebtedness to each other for the ways in which each has helped the other grow.

The new relationship changes the supervisor as well as the clinician. By becoming a supervisor of a supervisor, the supervisor is forced to move beyond previous levels of intimacy to dig deeper into self in order to share what supervision is about. By the process of articulating thoughts and feelings about supervision to another, the supervisor rediscovers and reintegrates the beliefs and values that moved him or her into supervisory work earlier.

This message has been implied throughout this book: Our lives reflect our relationships as much as our relationships reflect our individual lives, and good supervision is a example of this principle. The supervisory relationship has the power to transform both clinician and supervisor.

The learning process of supervision has its roots in your ability to envision what you, the clinician you supervise, and the relationship you have together can become. All the knowledge, skills, and techniques discussed here are merely tools for gathering, shaping, and translating your vision to others so that they may see what you see.

The learning process ends with the gift of vision. If you reflect on how others have helped you in the past, you may realize that what mattered in your relationships with mentors was not the advice they gave but the opportunity they provided for you to see something new inside yourself or in your future. By opening up to the vision you offer, the clinician begins to discover his or her own. The clinician's vision then both ripples out in an enlargening circle to influence the vision of others and ripples back to affect you. When our lives touch the lives of others, the circle becomes complete.

References

Alpher, V. S. (1991). Interdependence and parallel process: A case study of structured analysis of social behavior in supervision and short-term dynamic psychotherapy. *Psychotherapy, 28,* 218–231.

Bellah, R., Medsen, R., Swidler, A., & Tipton, S. M. (1985). *Habits of the heart.* New York: Harper and Row.

Castaneda, C. (1968). *The teachings of Don Juan: A Yaqui way of knowledge.* Berkeley, CA: University of California Press.

Duncan, B. (1988). Integrating individual and system approaches: Strategic-behavioral therapy. *Journal of Marital and Family Therapy, 14,* 151–162.

Ekstein, R., & Wallerstein, R. (1958). *The teaching and learning of psychotherapy.* New York: Basic Books.

Feldman, L. (1985). Integrative multi-level therapy: A comprehensive interpersonal and intrapsychic approach. *Journal of Marital and Family Therapy, 11,* 357–372.

Gottman, J. (1994, May–June). Why marriages fail. *Family Therapy Networker, 18,* 40–49.

Guy, J. D. (1987). *The personal life of the psychotherapist.* New York: John Wiley.

Kadushin, A. (1992). *Supervision in social work* (3rd ed.). New York: Columbia University Press.

Kahn, E. (1979). The parallel process in social work treatment and supervision. *Social Casework, 60,* 520–528.

Kottler, J. (1986). *On being a therapist.* San Francisco: Jossey-Bass.

Lebow, J. (1984). On the value of integrating approaches to family therapy. *Journal of Marital and Family Therapy, 10,* 127–138.

Lebow, J. (1987). Developing a personal integration in family therapy: Principles for model construction and practice. *Journal of Marital and Family Therapy, 13,* 1–14.

Mueller, W., & Kell, B. (1972). *Coping with conflict: Supervising counselors and psychotherapists.* New York: Appleton-Century-Crofts.

Reusch, J. (1961). *Therapeutic communication.* New York: W. W. Norton.

Simon, R., & Brewster, F. (1983, July–August). What is training? *Family Therapy Networker, 7,* 25–29.

Stanton, D. (1981). An integrated structural/strategic approach to family therapy. *Journal of Marital and Family Therapy, 7,* 427–440.

Stoltenberg, C. (1981). Approaching supervision from a developmental perspective: The counselor complexity model. *Journal of Counseling Psychology, 28,* 59–65.

Taibbi, R. (1980). *Client expectations and early discontinuance.* Unpublished paper. Columbia, SC: Family Service Center.

Taibbi, R. (1981). *Worker resistance: Fifty ways to leave your client.* Unpublished paper. Columbia, SC: Family Service Center.

Taibbi, R. (1990). Integrated family therapy: A model for supervision. *Families in Society, 7,* 542–549.